W9-DCX-379

## Praise for *Making Change Happen On Time, On Target, On Budget*

"Because our future will be challenged with continuous, impactful change, Matejka and Murphy's book is most timely and potentially invaluable."

—*Thomas J. Murrin, distinguished service professor, Duquesne University*

"Change is often challenging, especially in family businesses because of family dynamics. Matejka and Murphy have given us a map and tools to help us navigate through those challenges."

—*Rich Snebold, co-founder, The Family Business Center at Citizens; chairman, The Family Business Roundtable of Pittsburgh*

"This book successfully deals with perhaps the foremost growth-inhibiting issues in business today: recognizing, responding to, and managing dynamic marketplaces and organizations."

—*Ronald R. Morris, serial entrepreneur; Director of Entrepreneurial Studies, Duquesne University; host, "The American Entrepreneur" talk radio show*

# MAKING
# CHANGE
# HAPPEN

# MAKING
# CHANGE
# HAPPEN

## ON TIME
## ON TARGET
## ON BUDGET

*KEN MATEJKA* • *AL MURPHY*

Davies-Black Publishing
Mountain View, California

Published by Davies-Black Publishing, a division of CPP, Inc., 1055 Joaquin Road, Suite 200, Mountain View, CA 94043; 800-624-1765.

Special discounts on bulk quantities of Davies-Black books are available to corporations, professional associations, and other organizations. For details, contact the Director of Marketing and Sales at Davies-Black Publishing: 650-691-9123; fax 650-623-9271.

Visit the Davies-Black Publishing Web site at www.daviesblack.com.

The quotations sprinkled throughout this book were culled from the following volumes:

Anderson, J. B. *Speaking to Groups: Eyeball to Eyeball* (Vienna, Va.: Wyndmoor Press, 1989).
Bartlett, J. *Bartlett's Familiar Quotations* (New York: Permabook, 1953).
Boone, L. E. *Quotable Business*, 2nd ed. (New York: Random House, 1999).
Corey, M., and G. Ochoa. *The Man in Lincoln's Nose: Funny, Profound and Quotable Quotes of Screen Writers, Movie Stars, and Moguls* (New York: Simon & Schuster, 1990).
*Great Quotes on Wisdom* (New York: American Heritage, 1995).

09 08 07 06 05  10 9 8 7 6 5 4 3 2 1
Printed in the United States of America

**Library of Congress Cataloging-in-Publication Data**
Matejka, Ken.
Making change happen on time, on target, on budget / Ken Matejka and Al Murphy
— 1st ed.
p. cm.
Includes index.
ISBN 0-89106-190-8 (hardcover)
1. Organizational change. I. Matejka, Ken. II. Title.

FIRST EDITION
First printing 2005

*To my father, Joseph Matejka,*
*my sister, Mary Elizabeth Mawhinney,*
*and the memory of my mother, Mary Jula Matejka*
—KEN MATEJKA


*To my father, A. J. "Bud" Murphy Jr.,*
*and my wife, Laurel Brown Murphy*
—AL MURPHY

# CONTENTS

# ACTION TOOL EXERCISES

# TABLES

# FIGURES

# PREFACE

Welcome! We are pleased that you are looking at this book and considering reading it. Our purpose here is to set the tone and get you in the right frame of mind for leading change. In this preface, we will share with you our reasons for writing the book, describe the intended audience, give you a glimpse into our philosophy, and provide a quick preview of the remainder of the book.

Successfully leading organizational change can seem like an adventure, because it sometimes requires a skillful and delicate balance between extremes:

- Objectivity and subjectivity

- Logic and emotion

- Substance and style

- Big picture and details

- Right-brain and left-brain thought

- Art and science

Effective organizational changes should

- Start with the conviction that this change is correct and important

- Motivate the sponsors to do the careful and thoughtful preparation needed to create and sell a compelling change story

- Gain and maintain attention, interest, and ultimate commitment from everyone involved

- Convince everyone involved to take the desired constructive actions and make the change happen on time, on budget, and on target

One of the many ironies of being a competent change leader is that you (yourself) must be willing to change. Like it or not, every CEO, executive, manager, and supervisor is in the business of making change happen. Change starts with the one person you can control—yourself!

# WHO ARE WE TALKING TO, ANYWAY?

Like most books, this manuscript materialized from our needs, our clients' needs, and our MBA students' needs. None of the available books seemed to provide a systematic, logical, practical, reliable blueprint for coping with significant organizational changes.

Who should read this book? If you are looking for a quick fix, a "One-Minute Change Manager" approach, this book is not for you. Successful organizational change takes time, thought, commitment, and persistence.

In these turbulent times, many organizations are attempting massive changes to keep pace with their environments and competitors. These are the four potential audiences for this book:

- The **changers**—usually those executives at the top of the organization who are initiating strategic changes

- The **change managers**—those at the levels below the changers who have been (or will be) delegated the responsibility of being the primary implementers (project managers) for the changes

- The **positive changees**—those employees who are willing and able to help make the change successful

- The **students of leadership and change**—those who want to further develop their own change management skills

We hope that all four groups will find our suggestions useful.

In its broadest sense, this book should help anyone in business, the public sector, or the professions whose organization is in the midst of any of these efforts:

- Reacting to jolts and trends in the environment

- Transforming, reinventing, or strengthening itself

- Shifting its business strategy

- Creating a new work climate and culture

- Shoring up its internal capabilities

# AIN'T HINDSIGHT GRAND?

Waves of changes are pounding on our organizational shores. The ebb and flow are perpetual. Change is occurring at an increasing rate. It has been estimated that in the past twenty-five years, more knowledge and information have been obtained than existed in the entire prior history of planet Earth. What a time to be alive! If only we could see what is just over the horizon, how much better off we would be.

As evidence of just how difficult it is to see over the horizon, it might surprise and amuse you to learn that in 1899, the director of the U.S. Patent Office, Charles Duell, implied that maybe he should just close the office. He is quoted as saying, "Everything that can be invented has been invented." Whoa! Now that, with hindsight, is a really regrettable quote! For a little more fun, let's turn to two of our more current luminaries in the high-tech computer arena. These two quotes were culled from many "pratfalls" that appeared on November 23, 1999, in *USA Today:*[1]

> *There is no need for any individual to have a computer in their home.*
> —KEN OLSEN, DIGITAL EQUIPMENT CORPORATION, 1977

> *640K ought to be enough for anybody.*
> —BILL GATES, MICROSOFT, 1981

Those are curious quotes, aren't they? The names—Olsen and Gates—are impressive. We, with the luxury of 20/20 hindsight, can chuckle at these unfortunate mutterings. The future is apparently never totally visible, even to our best visionaries.

Rather than encouraging you to don your turban, gaze into your crystal ball, and play clairvoyant, in this book we supply a systematic process to successfully lead organizational change. We lay out a set of diagnostic tools to help you measure the importance of the critical variables (the external drivers of change and the internal organizational fitness), and we outline strategies for overcoming the common roadblocks to the successful implementation of change, along with some best practices of successful organizational change efforts. We also present two comprehensive tools—a change tracking map and a change tracking planner—that will help you get a grip on the process.

# WHAT IS OUR GREATEST CHALLENGE?

How would we describe this book? In the past two decades, we have spent most of our time teaching organizations how to lead change effectively—a truly daunting task! We have had some successes and some failures. This book represents the wisdom we have gleaned from all those experiences. Our consulting work has led us to two premises, which underlie our approach in this book:

- Most organizational changes are poorly implemented and therefore destined to fail (that is, not to be completed on time, on target, and on budget).

- Leading change is an essential business competence that can be learned!

We have valiantly tried to sprinkle this text with inspiring quotes, anecdotes, relevant and occasionally irreverent humor, and practical aids.

Most change books written in recent years have tended to be either dry texts (recounting research studies and written in theoretical terms) or practical books written in encyclopedic fashion, with no program, no glue. Our approach differs in several significant ways:

- We are more strategic than tactical.

- We present what we believe is a simpler, easier to remember, more practical, more user-friendly blueprint to use with different types of change.

- We explain the complexities of organizational change in a way that enables leaders to have a clear perspective or mind-set.

- We emphasize the assessment (analysis) phase of the business case for the change and the personal case for change—absolutely critical steps for successful implementation.

- We carefully explain five common potential barriers to successful implementation, coupled with suggested strategies to overcome each obstacle.

- We conclude by giving you format templates for use on each change launched.

# WHAT IS OUR MISSION?

It is our greatest hope that reading this book will help you

- Enlarge and focus your understanding of the organizational change process
- Enrich your understanding of and appreciation for change
- Improve your success rate in leading organizational changes
- Improve your change leadership skills
- Enhance your personal career potential and options
- Strengthen your organization's ability to successfully implement change

# YOU ARE ONE OF THE PERCEPTIVE PEOPLE

The fact that you are holding this book, even thinking about reading it, makes you one of the special people in organizations. You are an employee who is articulate, curious, ambitious, able, at least moderately willing to accept change, and concerned enough to distinguish between truth and fiction. You can, at times, spot the pattern in the chaos. You are one of those people who would really like to make organizations better places in which to work.

This book should help you participate more actively, more constructively, and more fully in the changing organizational world of tomorrow. Perceptive people aren't naive! They are hopeful and helpful in their capacity to overcome negativism, skepticism, helplessness, hopelessness, and resentment in organizations. Perceptive people know that successful organizational changes are a tantalizing mix of logic and magic.

# OUR PHILOSOPHY

As authors, we are advocates for the restoration and nurturing of the value that managers bring to the organizational dance. We strongly believe that managers can be helpfully involved and make valuable contributions without being consumed or cannibalized. We hope we have created a customer-friendly book—patterned but clear, simple, direct, and useful! We have tried to combine substance with style, theory with practicality, meaning with humor. We have tried to make each chapter a unique contribution to your tool kit.

# A PREVIEW OF COMING ATTRACTIONS

Chapter 1 sets the stage for the changing challenges that lie ahead.

Part One (Chapters 2–5) will help you build, articulate, and communicate a solid business case for your change.

Part Two (Chapters 6–11) will describe some different types of changes, explain how to manage the implementation of each type, and provide tools and advice for anticipating and reducing five potential barriers to the successful implementation of change.

The appendix gives you two summary tools to utilize for each change: the short, comprehensive "Change Tracking Map" to help you remember the important suggestions made throughout the book, and the "Change Tracking Planner" to use for each change launched. For fun, we have added the "Change Champions' Barometer" to give you a ballpark estimate of the probability that your change can or will be successfully implemented.

# ACKNOWLEDGMENTS

**Ken Matejka:** Many people contribute in many different ways to the completion of a book. First, I want to express my gratitude to my lovely and loving bride, Sally Carmichael Matejka; and to my beautiful and creative daughter, Anastasia Louise Matejka, an accomplished playwright. I truly appreciate their love, help, support, ideas, and sacrifices.

Thanks to Duquesne University for allowing me to take a sabbatical to work on this book.

A special thank you to Tom Murrin, Jim Stalder, and Richard J. Dunsing, who took time from their hectic schedules to review the original draft and share their wisdom. I also want to thank my Cranberry MBA class, especially Sue Dederer and Michaela Noakes, for their constructive criticism.

I want to thank my coauthor, Al (Punch) Murphy, for accepting the challenge of moving into unfamiliar territory to write this book with me and share his experiences and knowledge with a broader audience. That took courage.

**Al "Punch" Murphy:** My dad, A. J. "Bud" Murphy Jr., led me to the organization development field and a career in consulting. His integrity and values for helping, generosity, and persistence became tremendous gifts as I pursued my journey, and I am deeply grateful for all he has done. I was also very fortunate to study with some of the field's early founders—Dick Beckhard, Bob Tannenbaum, Shel Davis, Herb Shepherd, Mary Beth Peters, Marvin Wiesbord, Ed Schiene, Peter Vaill, and many others. To all my mentors, I am forever grateful for introducing me to their wisdom and the good path.

Laurel Brown Murphy shares in the challenges and work of our consulting business (Managing Change Consultants). Her support as CFO, soul mate, and horseback riding partner helps keep the spirit alive. Laurel's dedication to the business and support of this book is invaluable.

I also owe a debt of thanks to all my clients, graduate students, and workshop participants, who have challenged me and required me to build clarity of thought. A special thanks to Dan Holtz, Robert Parkinson, and John Sliwa for reviewing the original draft and sharing their wisdom.

And I thank Ken Matejka, who encouraged me to coauthor this book. His skill, experience, and initiative made this adventure possible.

# ABOUT THE AUTHORS

**Ken Matejka,** an award-winning educator, is currently professor of leadership and change management at the Donahue Graduate School of Business and the Palumbo School of Business Administration, Duquesne University. An active speaker, trainer, and consultant, he has delivered executive education courses and strategic retreats for leaders and change agents at such leading Fortune 500 companies as FedEx Ground, Dick's Clothing & Sporting Goods, AT&T, Sears Merchandising Group, and US Steel, several non-for-profit organizations, and numerous national associations. Author of five business books, including *A Manager's Guide to the Millennium,* his work also has appeared in many publications including *Business Horizons, Management Decision, Training, Executive Excellence, Working Woman,* and the *Dallas Morning News.*

**Al "Punch" Murphy,** principal of Managing Change Consultants, has concentrated on the issues associated with the implementation of change in organizations for more than thirty years. He received a master's degree in organization development from Pepperdine University and has studied and practiced with many of the leaders in the organization development field. Murphy has consulted with a variety of corporate, entrepreneurial, and not-for-profit clients including Mellon Financial, Highmark, Alcoa, Federal Express, and Citizens National Bank. He has served on the adjunct faculty at the Donahue Graduate School of Business at Duquesne University for more than ten years.

# Lead the Change Challenge

*The most distinguishing hallmark of the American society is and always has been change.*
—ERIC SEVAREID[1]

Completing a change on time, on budget, and on target actually begins with an educated, constructive perspective regarding the concept of organizational change. To begin to understand this concept, you need only take a look at some of its more or less recent history.

## CHANGE R US!

Since its birth as a nation, the United States has consistently been on the cutting edge of change. Why? Immigration, invention, and the belief in a better tomorrow. American society has historically welcomed change through generous immigration quotas. Wave after wave of prospective new U.S. citizens have more or less joyfully reached our shores and been welcomed into our society, sometimes swiftly, sometimes with some struggle, but all becoming part of the whole. Over the past two hundred years, the influx of new people

1

and cultures—Africans, Asians, Australians, Central Americans, Europeans, and South Americans—has created the most diverse nation on the face of Planet Earth.

America has also embraced change through invention and innovation (finding practical uses for the inventions). We have generally been the most creative nation in the world. Perhaps the immigration has led to the invention. Each new group brings different values, cultures, ideas, and perspectives and is motivated to achieve the American dream.

Our belief in possibilities—a better tomorrow—has further stimulated change. This belief in what could be is an optimistic, creative approach to life itself. We believe in ourselves, in the future, and in better horizons. Some cultures seem to suffer in relative silence—they do not feel deprived (or yearn for more) because they don't yet see the possibilities.

But even a country such as the United States, generally more comfortable with change than other nations, has occasionally seen its collective organizations caught off-guard, dwelling in the past, asleep at the switch!

## RIP VAN WINKLE AWAKES FROM HIS LITTLE NAP?

U.S. business in the late 1940s and early 1950s provides an interesting analogy and lesson regarding change on a national level. Immediately after World War II, U.S. industry found itself in a wonderful position. The United States was virtually the only industrial nation with its manufacturing base left totally intact. The war had destroyed much of the ability of England, France, Japan, Germany, Italy, and Russia to make products. When you combine this temporary monopoly with four years of pent-up worldwide demand for consumer goods, the result was a situation unbelievably rich in opportunity.

This was a booming time for U.S. companies. The business environment was relatively stable and changes were occurring slowly. Managing a business was much like drifting down a slow-moving river on a warm, sunny, windless day. Organizational behavior was relaxed and contemplative. Lean back. Catch some rays. Take a nap. It's good to be the king. With many of our oligopolies engaged in polite competition, whatever products our companies could produce could either be sold here or shipped overseas. The chief concern subtly switched from quality to volume. How can we make more faster? Don't get too hung up on little problems. Just ship the product! If something is wrong, they'll fix it over there when they get it. They need it now. Demand exceeded supply. Sales were abundant. Profits were bountiful. In this favorable and comparatively calm setting, planning was, compared to today, relatively simple and unhurried. For about twenty years, we slept like Rip Van Winkle. We were fat, happy, and content with the status quo.

## Who Are These Guys?

Innocently lurking on the horizon, however, was a rebuilding of the manufacturing bases of the war-torn countries. Slowly but surely, new products began to appear from new places. Gradually, our market shares began to erode. We didn't pay much attention at first. How can you take Japanese products seriously? The "made in Japan" label was considered the worst in the world at the time! Then, when it was a little late to respond quickly, we woke up, looked around, and scratched our organizational heads! Like Butch Cassidy and the Sundance Kid, we exclaimed—"Who are these guys?" A funny line? Humorous? More than that? The Japanese, with the help of Dr. W. Edwards Deming, (whose quality processes had been rejected by Detroit) were improving the quality of Japan's products slowly, consistently, continuously.

For a charming illustration of the business practicality of the phrase "Who are these guys?," consider the following anecdote, shared by Tom Murrin, a retired Westinghouse executive and a former member of the board of directors at Motorola (the leader in the cell phone industry at the time). At one board meeting, a board member walked in holding a small cell phone and exclaimed, "Who the heck is No-ki-a, and where are they? Sounds Japanese!" When told that Nokia was a new competitor, located in Finland, the board member remarked, "Finland? How can that be? There's nothing in Finland but ice and snow!"

Welcome to the new economy, where firms you never heard of, from places you aren't familiar with, can suddenly appear on your radar screens one day and steal your competitive advantage the next.

## Globalization Anyone?

One of the realities of the current business milieu is globalization. Of course, globalization couldn't just occur. A necessary precursor was a level of technological advancement. When technology exploded, leading to improvements in transportation and resulting in virtually free, instantaneous communication (you could communicate with anyone, anywhere, anytime for almost no cost), the stage was set for what's now called the "global economy." Prior to the introduction of faster airplanes, e-mail, faxes, and videoconferencing, how would you communicate with the plant manager in Belgium? Letters? (It's not called snail mail for nothing.) Telephone? (Expensive and unreliable.) Telex? (Pay by the word?) You get the point!

Fortunately, most U.S. manufacturing companies eventually awoke from their funk, developed new strategic initiatives, changed directions, and recovered rather well. Hopefully, our organizations have learned a lesson and will not be caught asleep at the switch any time soon.

## CAUTION: WHITE WATER AHEAD!

In his groundbreaking book *Future Shock,* Alvin Toffler suggested that the pace of change was accelerating. Reality has confirmed his assertion. In today's truly global economy, to use Peter Vaill's analogy, the organizational world is one of "permanent white water." The way to stay afloat now is to go into a "heads-up, sensing, searching, sorting, anticipating, adjusting, survival mode." Pay attention! Scan the environment. Gather information quickly and process it even faster. Your life depends on it. As external changes accelerate and competitive advantages shift, successfully leading change becomes an organizational imperative.

> *In a progressive country, change is constant; . . . change . . . is inevitable.*
> —BENJAMIN DISRAELI[2]

## THE CHANGING ORGANIZATIONAL LANDSCAPE

What is a better metaphor for today's organizations—*machines* or *living organisms?* As the world changes, external pressures continue to alter life inside our organizations. Have you noticed how the metaphors that we use to describe our organizational activities have modulated recently? Not long ago, we tended to depict organizations in engineering terms such as *fine-tuned machines.* Lately, we have begun to study and portray organizations as living, breathing organisms.[3] This shift from the physical to the biological metaphor is striking and illuminating. The physical state is constrained, even static. The biological state is one of continuous movement and change. As Darwin proposed in his *Origin of Species*, it is not necessarily the biggest or most powerful that survive, but those who are able to adapt. Adapt or die!

How do you get promoted to the top of an organization? The old metaphor of choice for career advancement was "climbing the corporate ladder." Have you noticed that you don't hear this metaphor as much in the new millennium? The corporate ladder has morphed into a rather crooked structure, with many missing rungs (due to corporate downsizings), confounded by cross-functional demands. A more apt metaphor for career advancement in the modern organization might be "mountain climbing." The right foothold is crucial to success. Failure has severe consequences. The path is not linear. Sometimes in mountain climbing, you may need to go sideways or even down in order to go up!

How do you lead organizational change in this baffling new environment? Perhaps the most dramatic and evident organizational changes are reflected in the fundamental leadership approaches and practices expected in organizations. Until recently, leadership, which was historically derived from military and religious institutions, was a command-and-control process. However, over the past two hundred years, modern society has been transformed from agricultural to industrial to service to informational. Currently, technological advances and the emerging global economy (where intense competition comes from strange new places) have even modified the practices of leadership. Leaders now talk in terms of visioning, sponsoring, enabling, championing, modeling, and empowering: a leader is no longer a ruler but a team advocate, someone who collaborates rather than disseminates, a champion and not a spokesperson, someone who doesn't control but empowers. These alterations are more than merely word shifts. Organizational changes have brought changes in what leaders do—how they spend their time. Furthermore, the changing demographics of customers and workforces have made "leading diversity" a valued new leadership skill. Diversity leads to complexity. Leading a diverse workforce aimed at serving diverse customers is challenging indeed! Of course, to be fair, some leadership practices have stood the test of time and change, but not many continue to survive or thrive.

How have the characteristics of economies and organizations changed? Remember the basic economics course you took? (Sorry. We didn't mean to depress you!) The valuable resources were typically expressed as land, labor, and capital. While these resources are still important, knowledge and information have become the precious, scarce commodities. Even our organizational

> *When a subject becomes obsolete, we make it a required course!*
> —PETER DRUCKER[4]

structures have experienced a migration from traditional hierarchies to self-organizing and often temporary project teams. Organizations are no longer built to resemble pyramids. They have become much flatter and more organic. In many industries, even the source and balance of power have shifted from producers to consumers. When we, as customers, can order almost anything, from almost any company, from almost anywhere, at almost any time, our expectations are raised.

Even the historic division-of-labor mentality in our organizations has given way to something akin to *Star Trek*'s Vulcan mind-melding. Economic constraints have been supplanted by creativity constraints.

Despite these fundamental alterations, many fading organizations desperately cling to their old ways. Change is very hard on many people and many organizations.

Here's one fine example of an organization clinging to the past: "It is characteristic of mankind to make as little adjustment as possible in customary ways in the face of new conditions; the process of social change is epitomized in the fact that the first Packard car body delivered to the manufacturer had a whipstock (a holder for your horse whip) on the dashboard."[5]

# THE ORGANIZATIONAL CHANGE PARADOX

Change can be a many-splintered thing! The organizational landscape is littered with the artifacts of defunct companies that couldn't implement important organizational changes. Why couldn't they pull it off? Why do most strategic organizational changes fail (come in, if at all, not on target, not on time, not on budget)? Why doesn't the vaccination take? Perhaps the many failures to implement organizational changes are partly due to the existing paradox and conflict between short-term productivity and long-term strategic change.

The dilemma is that in permanent white water, we must have time to learn how to navigate if we are to survive. But we don't have the time—we must react quickly or die. There is a great irony here. The way this paradox plays out in organizations is that when their environment is changing ever more quickly they must learn how to lead and manage in the new situations—they know this, but, from a practical business perspective, their managers are too busy fighting fires and responding to the financial analysts and stakeholder requests to do the necessary planning and set a new course.

> *There is more to life than increasing its speed.*
> —MOHANDAS K. GANDHI[6]

The organization must slow down (or even stop completely) in the short run to fix what is flawed, build the necessary capabilities, and learn the skills needed to go faster in the long run. (Would you really want to try to change a flat tire on a moving car?) You see, speed is not really the goal. Speed is a by-product of the application of skill. The goal is to build skill. As an example of this, consider the Watkins Glen road racing course speed record set by NASCAR driver Dale Earnhart Sr. When he set the record, Earnhart was coping with severe pain—he'd injured his ribs in a race the week before. The pain was so bad in the high-speed turns that he was forced to back off and find ways to smooth out each turn. He relied on his knowledge and experience. The irony is that on that twisting, turning racetrack, this backing-off approach allowed him to set the record for the fastest time ever run there. He slowed down and applied his skill, and the result was unprecedented quickness.

Like some of the executives we have worked with, you may have even more difficulty buying into and accepting this next issue. That's OK! Just consider the thought and try to understand the basic principle behind our last (we promise) racing analogy. Race car drivers tell us that while they must practice diligently and prepare themselves and their cars for the contest, in the actual race (assuming they are not attempting to set a land speed record) they would actually prefer to win at the slowest speed possible. Why? Because the faster they go, the more stress is placed on the car and the driver—the closer they come to a breakdown or crash! In organizations, people and equipment can break down when pushed too hard for too long. Organizational crashes occur when we lose control of our perspective, people, or processes—our speed exceeds our capabilities!

## THE PROCESS OF CHANGING

Consider this slightly different perspective. Maybe it isn't really the specific change that is critical, but the process of changing. As U.S. president and general Dwight David Eisenhower once said, the strategic plan may be meaningless, but strategic planning is invaluable. Eisenhower's planning principle can easily be applied to change. The process of changing requires people to anticipate, search, gather information, reason together, discover new methods for doing things, and interact in novel ways. This process of changing will change the participants forever. To say it another way, organizations that successfully change will be able to change again more easily and more quickly. They are building valuable new skills!

The true paradox of "success and change," as John L. Chambers said, is this: "We have to face the difficult challenge of changing when things are going well." Ah, now there's the real rub. We must learn to change when we are performing successfully. But success makes us cocky and content. Change is the antithesis of the much-loved maxim "If it ain't broke, don't fix it!" Another way to view this paradox is expressed in the old exercise proverb "no pain, no gain." First, organizations must be willing to change. But willingness depends on the belief that a change is necessary and that the proposal is the right change. In this case, the term *willingness* is meant to convey not obedience or compliance but a much deeper level of commitment and motivation.

The following statement may, at first, sound counterintuitive. *If you want to initiate a change in your organization, your first action should be to create dissatisfaction (pain) with the status quo.* If the employees are all content with the way things are, they won't be receptive to changes, will they? But if everyone shares the urgency of a strong perceived need to do things differently, you have a shot at successful change. This need for dissatisfaction to drive change is the reason that the assessment, articulation, and communication of the business case for change is such an important part of this book.

## THE CHANGE CHALLENGE PARADOX

One dilemma that is built into almost every organization is the pull-and-tug, the continuous trade-off that exists between the quest for immediate, continuous improvement in organizational efficiency and the necessity and allure of long-run strategic modifications. Pursuing both simultaneously is extremely difficult because strategic changes often bring short-run inefficiencies! Engineers are fond of saying that if you want efficiency, don't mess with a well-tuned process. The process has been sculpted, improved, honed to the point where it runs virtually error-free. Any strategic change, accompanied by the resulting tactical modifications, can potentially disrupt this delicate balance.

Of course, efficiency and strategy are both needed. Efficiency is a requirement for today's profits. Strategic change is a necessity for tomorrow's success. This paradox is further illustrated in Figure 1.

FIGURE 1
## The Change Paradox

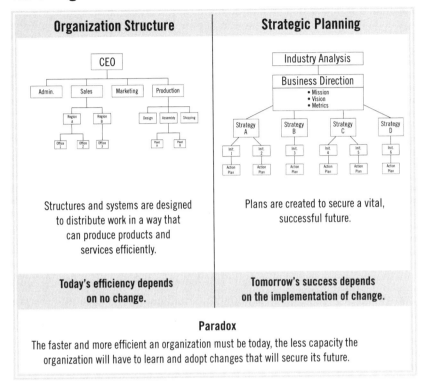

| Organization Structure | Strategic Planning |
|---|---|
| Structures and systems are designed to distribute work in a way that can produce products and services efficiently. | Plans are created to secure a vital, successful future. |
| **Today's efficiency depends on no change.** | **Tomorrow's success depends on the implementation of change.** |

**Paradox**

The faster and more efficient an organization must be today, the less capacity the organization will have to learn and adopt changes that will secure its future.

# BEWARE THE BLACK HOLE OF CHANGE!

Have you ever noticed how some strategic initiatives (changes) seem to vanish from the landscape? They fall into a "black hole," never to be heard from again. You can tell when a change has fallen into this abyss when some employee innocently asks, "Whatever happened to that initiative we started a year ago?" Nobody knows. Aha! That change has disappeared. It is our fervent hope that this book will help you reduce the number of organizational changes being sucked into the black hole of change.

# YA GOTTA LOVE CHANGE!

As Alvin Toffler asserted in *Future Shock,* our ability to invent things and then to innovate (devise and produce practical uses for inventions) far exceeds our societal and organizational ability to assimilate them. Assimilation lags—it takes time and skill. The same could be said for the successful implementation of change initiatives—they lag; they take time. Be prepared, be knowledgeable, be patient.

In the remainder of this book, we aim to provide you with the knowledge and skills needed to successfully lead change. We outline why the implementation of changes usually fails and what to do to improve your success rate, and we give you a step-by-step process to successfully implement your strategic initiatives.

Leading change is an extremely complex topic. The steps needed to succeed are numerous, probably infinite, but we have attempted to provide the most important elements throughout this book.

> *If you think you can or you think you can't, you're right!*
> —HENRY FORD[8]

Oh, by the way, sooner or later, the change will go off track. *Rerailing* the change and remotivating the people are also key capabilities.

This is an intriguing, exciting time to be alive and leading change. Change is bringing dark new dangers and marvelous new opportunities. Sniff them out! View changes with positive realism. Find the silver linings. Discern the patterns in the seeming chaos. Besides, you can't turn back the clock. Get over it. Move on. Learn to live with change. If you can, learn to love it.

## A FORMAT FOR SUCCESSFULLY LEADING CHANGE

Because of the countless critical variables, there is no one formula, no plastic overlay for successful change. Why not? Because the complexities dictate that one size does not fit all changes. However, our experience suggests to us that we can outline a process, a way of thinking and planning for successful change, that should significantly increase your organization's chances for success. That format is briefly presented in Table 1 and will be loosely followed throughout the book.

The significance of this format is simply this: organizations are too complex to permit a universal model that can explain all the dimensions, dynamics, reactions, and irrationalities related to every change. You must do the work—study the change, choose the approach, take the right actions for yourself. Our format will provide a reliable process for you to follow.

TABLE 1
# A Blueprint for Implementation

| Chapter | Leadership Capabilities |
|---|---|
| **Chapters 1–4:** Why change? | **Analyze:** Diagnose the sources and reasons for the change. Gather information.<br><br>**Establish a clear understanding of each change:** Do you really need to change? Why are you changing? What is driving this change? Why is this change the best choice? |
| **Chapter 5:** Develop and communicate a compelling business case for change | **Articulate:** Do your preparation carefully and thoughtfully, and clearly articulate and communicate your business case. How will you get buy-in? Why should this change successfully compete with the company's need for efficiency? |
| **Chapter 6:** Types of change | **Assess:** Identify the type of change and the implementation implications for that type. How should you lead this particular type of change? |
| **Chapter 7:** Culture and its impact on speed | **Appraise:** Examine the match between the change and the organizational culture. Given the degree of overlap, be realistic. How fast can you successfully implement this change? |
| **Chapters 8, 10, and 11:** Dealing with individual resistance, silos, and resources | **Anticipate:** Evaluate and prioritize the potential roadblocks to this change. Where will the resistance to this change originate? How can you act in advance to reduce or overcome the resistance? |
| **Chapter 9:** Sponsoring change | **Act:** Make sound decisions. Employ the best leadership practices. What can you do to sponsor the change and shepherd it to a successful conclusion—on time, on target, on budget? |

# THE BOTTOM LINE

As the old joke goes—the good news is that accelerating change is here to stay. And the bad news is that accelerating change is here to stay. People are changing. Organizations are changing. Technology is changing. Society is changing. Legislation is changing. Why not join the new economy and acquire the new skills needed to prosper? Don't be satisfied with the status quo—the status quo is an illusion, a temporary condition built on historical numbers. Learn to be dissatisfied with success. Teach others to be dissatisfied and embrace change. Most important, learn how to change when things are going well. We wrote this book because we firmly believe that successfully leading organizational change efforts is a skill that can be learned!

Thanks for joining us. The adventure begins. . . .

# BUILD THE BUSINESS CASE FOR CHANGE

Change? What change? Why are we changing? When an organizational change is announced, it is reasonable for employees to ask, "What's up now?" They have a lot more questions than answers. Typically, a change comes as somewhat of a surprise to the bulk of the workforce. They have legitimate concerns. Has management done its homework? Has this change been thoroughly researched? Is this change really needed? Is this the right change? To jump-start the initial understanding and eventually gain buy-in for the change, management must be able to justify it logically and persuasively.

The first major chunk of this book (Chapters 2–5) relates to building and communicating the change story.

We believe that change comes from three main sources:

- External environmental pressures and the competitive situation

- Business strategy set by the CEO and top team

- Desire to enhance the organization's internal fitness

A clear understanding of these three drivers is the foundation needed to construct a believable justification for the change and help you select the right change for your organization.

Chapter 2 demonstrates the importance of environmental scanning to identify the potential external sources for the change. Chapter 3 examines the organization's business strategy as the second potential force for launching the change. Chapter 4 explores the final potential driver, the pressures coming from the organization's desire to enhance its internal fitness and become more competitive. Finally, Chapter 5 examines the communication steps needed to tell the change story to the organization's members effectively.

## SELECTING THE RIGHT CHANGE

Face it, if you choose to implement the wrong strategic initiative, this book will be of marginal value. Charging expertly down the wrong path is still organizational suicide! For example:

- You could be manufacturing quality buggy whips, typewriters, black-and-white TVs, telephone lines, or audiocassette tapes and not developing new products to replace them as they become obsolete.

- You could be moving toward fragmentation when consolidation is needed.

- You could be building organizational pyramids when flexibility and response time are becoming crucial.

- You could be making an unfortunate acquisition.

- You could be emphasizing cost-cutting when your customers are crying out for better service.

Tastes change. Technology advances. Markets expand. Markets contract. Markets shift. Pyramids get flattened. Suppliers get outsourced. The Internet beckons. Globalization intensifies. Choose carefully!

The importance of selecting the right change is relatively apparent because no manager or organization can afford the huge costs of pursuing and implementing the wrong change. The price of lost opportunities, lost time, lost momentum, damaged personal credibility, spent political favors, broken promises, and squandered resources often precludes successfully sponsoring another change in that organization, at least for a long time to come.

In one organization where one of us was consulting, a sponsor was selected to implement a marketing strategy for a new product. The new product had extensive costs associated with getting it ready for sale. About a year after launch, it was discovered that the wrong market had been targeted. The losses incurred led the CEO to abandon the product and lose confidence in the sponsor. The mistake was so damaging to the sponsor's reputation that he decided to make a career change. The people who participated in the implementation of the marketing strategy were all reassigned with little chance of ever participating in new product introduction again.

You can learn from your mistakes. But these lessons learned the hard way are costly because of the risk-averse atmosphere that results. There is no substitute for selecting the right strategic change from the get-go.

## IMPORTANT QUESTIONS TO ASK ABOUT THE RIGHT CHANGE

We can't tell you what change to make. You knew that! We don't know your industry, your competition, or your people the way you do. What we can do is suggest some questions that you should be asking yourself regarding any strategic change.

As one of the quotes we used earlier suggests, changing when things are going well is the litmus test. Most great organizations are constantly changing, always looking for new and better ways to do things. Still, before you make a change, it would be prudent to ask the following questions:

**Is this change really necessary?** Is the implementation of this change vital to gaining or maintaining a sustainable competitive advantage? Should you just do what you already do, only better? Stick to your knitting? For example, Costco Wholesale Corporation has continued to focus single-mindedly on selling goods at the lowest possible price for the past twenty years, with no exceptions allowed. The result has been tremendous growth, and Costco is the only firm to successfully challenge Wal-Mart. Its leaders have passed up lots of opportunities to make lots of changes.[1]

**What is driving this perceived need for change?** Is the driver external or internal? Are you heading into the unknown? Are you following others?

**Would successful implementation really achieve the desired results?** What would the change accomplish? Have you clearly identified and articulated a measurable objective for the change? Will this change solve the issues and problems? Have you anticipated the new issues and problems that this change will bring?

**Is a better choice available?** Have you creatively brainstormed and explored all the possibilities? Have you been able to detect any emerging patterns in your industry? Why is this change the best option?

**Realistically, can your organization successfully implement this change?** Does this change align with the organizational culture? Does your organization have the skills and resources needed? What is the history of change efforts in your organization? Is the change responding to past, present, or future trends? What is the probability for successful implementation? (See the "Change Champions' Barometer" in the appendix.)

> *You shouldn't take a fence down until you know the reason it was put up.*
> —G. K. CHESTERTON[2]

**Is this change worth the costs?** Have you clearly identified the benefits and costs of making this change? Do the benefits clearly outweigh the possible costs (money, resource utilization, psychic drain). What are the opportunity costs?

There are strategic changes and then there are *strategic changes*. Some changes are obvious. They appeal to logic and intuition and need no further analysis. Other transitions carry an expense and risk that require the careful consideration we offer throughout this book. It is the riskier changes that make a great argument for test-driving. Some strategic changes lend themselves to test marketing, pilots, or laboratory experiments that help answer the question, Have we selected the right change to make?

One final disclaimer is needed here. Have a little patience. Don't forget, truly visionary leaders and changes will initially be scoffed at, misunderstood, fought tooth and nail. Someday, two or three years from now, when the others finally get it, they will jump on board.

# Examine the External Pressures Driving Change

*Companies that learn to manage change are in the best position to continue to take the risks needed to stay out in front.*
—MICHAEL S. DELL[1]

Is it just us, or does Planet Earth seem to be spinning (changing) a little faster these days? For example, most young men and women entering college this year have always had computers and computer games at their disposal. The Internet is something they take for granted. Some employees can't remember not having a desktop or laptop computer. Yet it has been only twenty years since desktop and laptop computers became commonplace in homes, schools, and businesses.

Only a few years ago, if we suggested to you that scientists would soon be able to clone human beings and that organizations might eventually clone their best workers, you probably would have laughed at us and accused us of being in the Twilight Zone somewhere. Cloning isn't outrageous or improbable anymore—or funny.

Not long ago, if we had suggested to you that millions of U.S. jobs would be outsourced to India or China, or that most people would be walking around (and driving) with a cell phone pressed against one ear, you probably would have ridiculed our idea. Isn't it possible that in the near future, cell phones will be miniaturized and surgically attached? Perhaps incoming college freshmen will get chip implants behind their ears containing all the information in the Library of Congress and they will access the information via neural waves. Or maybe Microsoft, Disney, and MIT will form a strategic alliance to deliver higher education to the world? Anyway, to echo Bob Dylan, the times really are changing now.

# WHY BOTHER IDENTIFYING THE SOURCE FOR THE CHANGE?

Chapters 2 through 4 address three separate potential sources for a change. But you might well be asking, Why should anyone bother analyzing the sources of the change they are trying to implement? Who cares where the pressure for the change is coming from? Well, we are advising you to begin your change initiative analysis by pinpointing the source of the change for several very good reasons. First, identifying the source of the pressure to make the change helps you answer the question in almost every employee's mind: Why are we making this change anyway? For example, compare the probable reaction to something generic and unappealing, such as "We must do it to survive," to the way people would respond to a statement like this: "The pressure to implement this change is coming from our competition. Three of our four major competitors are offering this service and we estimate that we have lost 5.2 percent of our sales in the past six weeks ($2.2 million) because we don't currently offer the service!" Now, isn't that answer a lot more informed and powerful? Who cares where the pressures for change are coming from? The people who have to implement the change care, that's who!

Second, you may reevaluate the need for the change once you discover the source. For example, perhaps the pressure for this change is coming from a small but vocal market segment—a segment that your organization has been consciously and strategically moving away from in the past six months. All of a sudden, you may realize you don't need to make the change after all, and that will make life that much easier.

And third, uncovering the source may lead to the acknowledgment that a different change is needed. For example, say you're leading a car company that is reacting to new federal guidelines regarding average miles per gallon for its fleet of automobiles by attempting to lower (change) the weight of the cars. Simultaneously, the company might be working on another change that improves emissions performance but increases the weight of each car. What about alternatives (changes) that accomplish both objectives simultaneously? Perhaps the change the company should be attempting is an intermediate to long-range strategy emphasizing the development of hybrid engines? Natural gas cars? Battery-assisted drive trains? Hydrogen fuel cells? These changes might be much better solutions that treat the problem (continually higher levels of air pollution initiating stricter automobile emission standards) rather than the symptoms (reacting to two conflicting legislative edicts). The source for this change is the growing air pollution problem, not the legislation that attempts to address it.

We hope you are beginning to see the relevance of clearly discerning the source of pressure for the change.

## IDENTIFYING THE EXTERNAL DRIVERS OF CHANGE

One primary source for organizational change is the external environment.[2] In fact, an assessment of the environmental shifts (outside the organization) is the primary building block in constructing a clear understanding of why you are introducing this change. If you don't build, articulate, and communicate a strong business case for the specific change, obtaining buy-in from affected employees will be much more difficult. Employees want to know why they are working to make any change. Generic pronouncements accompanying a change—"Well, if we don't do this, we won't be profitable"—aren't well received because they are vague and therefore not very convincing, let alone compelling. There must be hundreds of changes a company could make to become more profitable. Why this change? Why now?

Most of the dramatic shifts taking place in the external environment will, sooner or later, have an impact on your organization. The timing, intensity, and organizational results of a specific environmental change will differ from industry to industry. For example, the retail clothing industry is relatively susceptible to consumer trends compared to, say, utilities, which are more heavily regulated and therefore affected more by legislative actions.

A great place to start your analysis of the need for changes in your organization is to appraise new developments occurring in the broader environment and to gauge the potential impact of specific changes on your industry in general and your organization in particular. This information is critical to help you

- Pinpoint the relative new opportunities and threats emerging in the external environment

- Understand the direct links between the external pressures and the suggested internal changes

- Anticipate the impact the external change may have on your organization and the appropriate response level needed

- Begin to craft your business case to educate your employees about why this change is needed, what the change will accomplish, and what happens if you and they don't change

Table 2 suggests some possible drivers of change and the potential impacts they are having on organizations. Although the structure of the table is somewhat arbitrary, we have chosen to divide the external environment into the following broad areas:

- Competitive pressures and customer expectations

- Technological advancements

- Social trends, economic cycles and adjustments, and regulatory pressures

A clear comprehension of the potential external pressures is the starting point to successfully analyze the change. As you peruse Table 2, ask yourself these questions:

- Which changes are critical foreshadowers of how your organization will be doing business tomorrow?

- How are these alterations likely to play out in your industry?

- How will they play out in your organization?

- How can you seize veiled opportunities?

- How could your organization get ahead of the curve and turn a potential threat into an opportunity?

TABLE 2
# External Drivers of Change

| | Examples of Drivers | Examples of Organizational Changes |
|---|---|---|
| | **Industry Drivers** | |
| **Competitive Pressures** | • Competitive advantages<br>• Emerging economies<br>• Industry consolidation<br>• Industry fragmentation<br>• New entrants<br>• Narrowing differentiation<br>• Shareholder value | • Acquisitions<br>• Joint ventures<br>• Strategic alliances<br>• Cost reduction<br>• Lean production techniques<br>• Product development<br>• Outsourcing<br>• Reengineering<br>• Supply chain management |
| **Customer Expectations** | • Changing buyer behavior<br>• Customer value search<br>• Global markets<br>• Rising standards<br>• Search for variety<br>• Search for customization<br>• Service requirements<br>• Convenience requirements<br>• Jumping on bandwagon (fad) | • Customer feedback systems<br>• Customer focus groups<br>• Microsegmentation<br>• Mass customization<br>• "Smart" products<br>• 24/7 availability<br>• Shorter time to market<br>• Faster turnaround |

TABLE 2 (cont'd)

| | Examples of Drivers | Examples of Organizational Changes |
|---|---|---|
| | **Technology Drivers** | |
| **Technological Advancements** | <ul><li>Faster, cheaper transportation</li><li>Replacing labor cost with technology</li><li>Instant information and communication</li><li>Narrowcasting</li><li>E-commerce</li><li>Artificial intelligence</li><li>Information systems</li><li>CAD/CAM</li><li>DNA mapping</li></ul> | <ul><li>Data mining</li><li>Electronic monitoring and sensors</li><li>Virtual organizations</li><li>Telecommuting options</li><li>New security system</li><li>Robotic applications</li><li>Intranets</li><li>Miniaturization of products</li><li>Innovative distribution and delivery techniques</li></ul> |
| | **Environmental Drivers** | |
| **Social Trends** | <ul><li>Demographics</li><li>Immigration issues</li><li>Employment trends</li><li>Workforce diversity</li><li>Terrorism</li></ul> | <ul><li>Lifelong learning</li><li>Knowledge entrepreneurs</li><li>Flextime scheduling</li><li>Cross-functional teams</li><li>Ethics and social responsibility</li><li>Retention strategies</li><li>Diversity training</li></ul> |

TABLE 2 (cont'd)

| | Examples of Drivers | Examples of Organizational Changes |
|---|---|---|
| | **Environmental Drivers (continued)** | |
| **Economic Cycles and Adjustments** | ▪ Capital market pressures<br>▪ Currency fluctuations<br>▪ Business cycles<br>▪ Interest rates<br>▪ Political/ideological collapses<br>▪ Labor supply and demand | ▪ Hedging investments<br>▪ Direct foreign investments<br>▪ Redefining political risk<br>▪ Balanced portfolios |
| **Regulatory Pressures** | ▪ Intellectual property laws<br>▪ Tariffs<br>▪ EEOC<br>▪ Affirmative action<br>▪ NAFTA<br>▪ Americans with Disabilities Act<br>▪ Industry Regulation/ Deregulation | ▪ Political lobbying<br>▪ Diversity training<br>▪ Management and development coaching<br>▪ Risk management strategies<br>▪ New audit strategies |

Because the external environment is such a broad, complicated topic, we have tried to simplify it by structuring Table 2 in a user-friendly way. Of course, when we simplify, we risk errors of omission. Table 2 is not an exhaustive representation of all that is happening in the external arena. Think of it as a starting point, a think piece to help you begin to contemplate the events taking hold in the world and how these developments may be affecting your organization. Familiarize yourself with the contents. Feel free to add, delete, or modify items. Customize the external environment to fit your organization and your industry.

## Competitive and Customer Pressures

Competitive and customer pressures are driving changes in modern organizations. For example, globalization has brought more competitors and fiercer competition. Some industries are consolidating, while others are fragmenting. Cheap labor from developing countries has caused cost reductions, job migrations, and the resulting price pressures. Reduced costs, reflected in lower prices, have transformed some differentiated products into commodities and resulted in organizational impacts such as downsizing and outsourcing. Competitive pressures have also resulted in acquisitions, mergers, and strategic alliances.

*We were fairly arrogant, until we realized the Japanese were selling quality products for what it cost us to make them.*
—PAUL A. ALLAIRE[3]

Customers are changing too. Customer expectations are rising. The convenience and choices of Internet buying, selling, and delivery have elevated consumer expectations for prices, quality, service, variety, and convenience. Retail customers have become more savvy, price-conscious shoppers. Increasing competition is raising the expectations of industrial consumers in similar ways.

## Technological Advancements

As we mentioned in Chapter 1, the phenomenon known as globalism would not have materialized without the technological advancements in communication. Prior methods were costly, time-consuming, and often unreliable.

*Before you build a better mousetrap, it helps to know if there are any mice out there.*
—MORTIMER B. ZUCKERMAN[4]

On another front, tracking systems have allowed firms like UPS and FedEx to deliver packages anywhere in the world, on schedule, and have provided precise package location during transit for both senders and recipients.

## Social, Economic, and Regulatory Pressures

Social trends, economic variables, and new legislation also apply pressure for change in today's organizations. For example, a social trend toward more nutritional foods has caused McDonald's to offer a salad selection at its restaurants.

*I don't set trends. I just find out what they are and I exploit them.*
—DICK CLARK[5]

Rising interest rates can cause postponement of plant construction. Job sharing, flextime, and even day care are becoming more common because of social trends toward both partners working.

On the legislative front, deregulation has transformed some industries and forced several excellent service firms to reluctantly learn how to market their products and services in a competitive environment. AT&T is a good example.

## A PRACTICAL TOOL TO DETERMINE EXTERNAL PRESSURES FOR CHANGE

To turn this discussion into a more practical how-to for your organization, you need a tool. To help you identify the prominent external pressures that your organization is most likely to encounter, we have provided the "External Drivers of Change Survey" (Action Tool 1) as a guide. Fill it out to determine what you perceive to be the important issues for your organization. Modify the questions to make it more germane to your circumstances. Use it with your direct reports to brainstorm environmental possibilities and make contingency plans for organizational impacts.

Your summary (total number of 1's) for each of the external drivers (competitive pressures and customer expectations, technological advances, and social trends, economic cycles and adjustments, and regulatory pressures) should give you a good indication of where you believe external pressures are likely to originate for your organization.

## ASSESSING EXTERNAL FACTORS

If you are currently planning a significant change in your organization, to what extent do external pressures drive it? Answer the questions in Action Tool 2 to find out.

ACTION TOOL 1

## External Drivers of Change Survey

**Directions:** Place a number beside each statement according to how true and relevant it is for your organization.

**Rating Key**
1 = Causing significant pressure for change
2 = Causing some pressure for change
3 = Is not a pressure today

_____ 1. We have competitors who produce the same quality at a lower cost.

_____ 2. We are contemplating a major systems conversion.

_____ 3. We anticipate that a significant portion of our workforce will telecommute.

_____ 4. Our competitors and customers are creating pressure to deliver significantly faster.

_____ 5. New technology is causing a significant number of systems changes.

_____ 6. Pending federal legislation may dramatically change our industry.

_____ 7. We are expanding our exporting activity outside the domestic United States.

_____ 8. We are committing significant resources to our e-commerce initiative.

_____ 9. Our industry is in the process of deregulation or about to deregulate.

_____ 10. The number of competitors or substitute products is driving prices and margins down.

_____ 11. We currently are adopting virtual office techniques.

_____ 12. Qualified labor at an affordable cost is very difficult to attract and retain.

_____ 13. Our customers are demanding more and better at a lower cost.

_____ 14. We are at a disadvantage when it comes to equipment efficiency.

_____ 15. Our sales follow the general economic cycles in the U.S. economy.

_____ 16. We are merging two organizations as a result of an acquisition.

_____ 17. Economics of scale drive change in our industry.

_____ 18. Managing our organization has become significantly more complex.

_____ 19. Alliances and joint ventures are becoming critical to the success of organizations in our industry.

_____ 20. We are creating a data warehouse for future marketing initiatives.

_____ 21. Our sales are significantly affected by foreign economic cycles.

ACTION TOOL 1 (cont'd)

---

## Summarizing Your Survey

**Directions:** Place the values you gave for each question on the survey in the spaces below and total the number of "1" ratings in each category.

### Competitive Pressures and Customer Expectations

| | | | |
|---|---|---|---|
| 1. Lower cost | _____ | 13. Customer demand | _____ |
| 4. Faster delivery | _____ | 16. Acquisition | _____ |
| 7. Exports | _____ | 19. Alliances | _____ |
| 10. Lower margins | _____ | **Total number of 1's** | _____ |

### Technological Advances

| | | | |
|---|---|---|---|
| 2. System conversion | _____ | 14. Obsolete equipment | _____ |
| 5. New technology | _____ | 17. Economies of scale | _____ |
| 8. E-commerce | _____ | 20. Data warehouse | _____ |
| 11. Virtual office | _____ | **Total number of 1's** | _____ |

### Social Trends, Economic Cycles and Adjustments, and Regulatory Pressures

| | | | |
|---|---|---|---|
| 3. Telecommuting | _____ | 15. U.S. economy | _____ |
| 6. Legislation | _____ | 18. Management | _____ |
| 9. Deregulation | _____ | 21. Foreign economies | _____ |
| 12. Labor supply | _____ | **Total number of 1's** | _____ |

ACTION TOOL 2

## Determining the Impact of External Factors

**Directions:** To what extent are external factors at the root of reasons to implement this key action? Circle the percentage below that you think is most appropriate to answer this question. Next, check the appropriate box to indicate the main source of pressure for this change. Finally, write a few sentences to describe some of the specific details.

0%   10%   20%   30%   40%   50%   60%   70%   80%   90%   100%

### Describe the Source for Change

**Which factor?**

☐ Competition ☐ Social Trends
☐ Customers ☐ Economy
☐ Technology ☐ Regulation

**What are the details?**

_____

_____

_____

_____

# THE BOTTOM LINE

No organization operates in a vacuum. Some organizational changes are being driven by factors in the external environment, and it is imperative to react to them. Clearly identifying the external pressures (sources) for a specific organizational change is the all-important first step in being able to correctly understand and articulate the need for action inside the organization, and to communicate that need effectively. Remember, the people who have to implement the change or will be inconvenienced by it do care about what is causing the change!

# 3

# Understand the Business Strategy Driving Change

*If we don't change direction, we're*
*likely to end up where we're headed.*
—CHINESE PROVERB

To stand out among its competitors, your organization must be able to do something better than anyone else. A second source of significant change for organizations comes straight from the CEO and the senior management team. Those executives at the top level have the responsibility to assure the long-term vitality and competitiveness of the enterprise. To fulfill this responsibility, top management must create a vision, strategy, and goals. Additionally, the top team needs adequate industry intelligence about competitors, customers, technology advancements, regulatory change, and social trends to position their company for future success. When the source of change is the business plan, the top management team is driving change.

Strategic planning normally results in strategies to achieve some type of sustainable competitive advantage. We have enhanced Michael Porter's original model of competitive advantage (constructed at Harvard University) to help you clarify this quest for advantage. (See Table 3.) Porter's premise is that organizations within an industry have only a handful of ways to set themselves apart from the pack so that customers will perceive their product or service as creating greater value than the competition's. Every organization needs to build some kind of sustainable edge that, in the eyes of the customer, separates it from competing companies. Two kinds of strategies, *differentiation* and *scale*, enable a company to do this. In this chapter, we describe three differentiation strategies—customer service, product attributes, and niche markets— and two scale strategies—cost orientation and market dominance. Table 3 illustrates these strategies.

TABLE 3
## Achieving Competitive Advantage[1]

| | Outperform | Outsmart |
|---|---|---|
| | **Differentiation Strategies** | |
| | Customer Service | Product Attributes |
| **Customer Orientation** | ■ Ritz Carlton, British Airlines, Nordstrom<br>■ **Goal:** Customer loyalty<br>■ **Strategy:** The customer is always right. | ■ Sony TV, pharmaceuticals, 3M<br>■ **Goal:** Price premium through innovation<br>■ **Strategy:** Create a better mousetrap! |
| | **Niche Markets**<br>■ Harley-Davidson, Ben & Jerry's, Rolex, Cabela's<br>■ **Goal:** Unique market segment leader<br>■ **Strategy:** Focus on segment. | |
| | **Scale Strategies** | |
| | Cost Orientation | Market Dominance |
| **Competitor Orientation** | ■ Gasoline, corn/wheat, generic drugs<br>■ **Goal:** Low-cost provider<br>■ **Strategy:** Pursue continuous improvement and new technology. | ■ Coke, Microsoft, Home Depot, Wal-Mart<br>■ **Goal:** Market shaper<br>■ **Strategy:** Keep growing market share. |

# DIFFERENTIATION STRATEGIES

One way to put some daylight between your organization and the competition is to be so different from your competitors that customers are attracted to the superior nature of your products or services. In our experience, companies have three ways to achieve competitive advantage through differentiation—outperform competitors through superior customer service, outsmart them by developing unique product attributes, or appeal to a specific market segment using a niche strategy.

## Provide the Best Customer Service

Successfully setting yourself apart from the competition requires knowing what your customers want and then outperforming your rivals. The goal is to provide such excellent service that it results in strong customer loyalty. These satisfied customers not only provide repeat business but also enthusiastically refer your business to others. They become (as Ken Blanchard writes) your "raving fans." Some examples of companies that have successfully achieved this service excellence are Ritz Carlton, British Airlines, Nordstrom, and the Disney theme parks. It is not unusual to hear and read the stories about how these companies have "delighted" patrons in some unusual way.

Ritz Carlton is a multiple winner of the Malcolm Baldrige Award and of the J. D. Powers service awards. The elements of the Ritz Carlton strategy include an advanced customer information system that records individual customer preferences, delegation that empowers all employees to solve customer problems (in real time), significant customer relations training, and impeccable facilities management. Ritz Carlton's investment in infrastructure to support excellent service allows it to charge its premium price while retaining its "raving fans."

> *The dollar bills that customers get from their tellers in four banks are the same; what is different, are the tellers.*
> —STANLEY MARCUS[2]

Another great example of a firm providing superior customer service is a regional grocery chain called Ukrop's, operating in the Tidewater area of Virginia and North Carolina. Founded on the Golden Rule, Ukrop's has the cleanest stores, the best produce, the friendliest employees, and an unbelievable community image. Unlike its competitors, Ukrop's is not open on Sundays (the Sabbath), closes at 10 p.m. each evening (so employees can be with their families), and doesn't sell beer and wine (unlike other grocers). Despite these decisions (or perhaps because of them), Ukrop's has been extremely profitable and generously philanthropic. Oh, by the way, its leaders have fought the tendency to expand nationally because they don't believe they can maintain this same level of service if they become too large.

## Build Better Mousetraps

A second way to set a company apart from its competitors (using a differentiation strategy) is to have uniquely superior product attributes. Make products and services that are clearly better than your competitors' from a feature and function perspective. This strategy also requires knowing what your customers' wants are and then creatively crafting a superior product and service design. Rather than outperforming your competitors, here you are trying to outsmart them. The goal of this strategy is to command segment leadership so that the superior product or service can command a price premium. Customers are willing to pay for products or services that have superior qualities or value.

> *If a man writes a book, preaches a better sermon, or makes a better mousetrap than his neighbor, though he build his house in the woods, the world will make a beaten path to his door.*
> —RALPH WALDO EMERSON[3]

Some examples of companies that have successfully achieved product attribute differentiation are Sony TV, 3M, and pharmaceuticals. This strategy leads many companies to claim to have the best product, but few have genuinely created the attributes that set them apart. As an example, all airline carriers claim to be the best at something, but a clear-cut differentiation was the Concorde supersonic transport's ability to cross the ocean in two hours, thus eliminating some of the issues related to jet lag. No other airline could match that attribute—or charge Concorde's rates. When Federal Express promised to have your package delivered in one day, no other competitor could match that promise. When 3M invented Post-it adhesive, no other competitor could duplicate its "no permanent stick" feature.

## Carve Out Your Special Piece of the Pie

The final way to differentiate your organization from your competitors' is called a niche strategy. Smaller companies don't have the resources that large companies do. Companies pursuing a niche strategy identify and focus on smaller market segments and produce products and services that appeal to those unique markets. The goal is to provide a more informed, personal touch that makes customers feel special because they identify with the image associated with the product or service.

Some examples of companies that we believe have successfully carved out a unique market niche are Harley-Davidson, Ben & Jerry's, Rolex, Mont Blanc, Rolls Royce, L. L. Bean, and Cabela's. These companies are not neces-sarily competing on the basis of product attribute or service; instead, they are setting themselves apart based on lifestyle and an affinity with some special set of values. It could be said Harley-Davidson's niche is the outlaw image; Ben & Jerry's niche is the socially and environmentally responsible community; and Cabela's niche is the purist outdoor recreation enthusiast.

> *The underdog in many products . . . can pick and choose where it wants to hit the giant; the giant, by contrast, must defend itself everywhere.*
> —GEORGE H. LESCH[4]

Elements of the Harley-Davidson strategy include a patented sound from the motorcycles' exhaust, apparel consistent with the outlaw image, and organized rides and club and social events. All these elements have the goal of making customers feel that they are special members of the affinity group because they own a Harley.

# SCALE STRATEGIES

A second type of strategy applicable for setting a company apart from the pack is to achieve a level of volume or size that allows you to set your prices below the competition's. Customers are attracted to your firm because of savings or the stability of the brand name.

In our view, companies have two possible ways to promote this size advantage.

## Provide the Lowest Price

Be the low-cost producer! Low cost and low price usually become a significant issue when your product is viewed as a commodity. Despite Tom Peters's assertion that you can differentiate anything, it's tough to differentiate a product that has no real distinguishing features other than price—that is, a commodity. When you buy your cereal, do you care whether the wheat, corn, or rice was grown in Arkansas, Kansas, or China? Probably not. Crops are usually considered commodities. When you stop at a gas station to fill up your automobile's tank, do you care if the oil from which the gas was made was extracted in Pennsylvania, Venezuela, Saudi Arabia, or the Republic of Russia? We doubt it. Oil is a commodity. What you care about is the price you pay. When the Chinese can deliver carbon on-site for less than the fixed costs of an American firm, how much more are you willing to pay for the perception of quality? Or has carbon become a commodity?

Commodity companies, unable to clearly differentiate their products based on consumer perceptions of superior attributes or performance, are usually forced to turn their attention to price to attract customers.

> *I found the greater the volume, the cheaper I could buy and the better value I could give customers.*
> —FRANK W. WOOLWORTH[5]

To offer the lowest prices, companies must be the low-cost producers. Only then can significant price flexibility be an option. In a commodity industry, the company that can produce at the lowest cost has a competitive advantage.

Some common strategies used by low-cost providers include lowering unit cost by achieving economies of scale (volume production); installing efficient (and volume discounted) supply chain management; continually improving production processes (including lean production techniques that eliminate waste); and outsourcing noncore competencies. A clear example of an industry that has adopted these strategies is big agriculture. These same economies of scale are not available to small family-farm producers.

## Be the 800-Pound Gorilla

The other scale strategy that could be employed to set your company apart from the competition is sheer growth and size. Grow! Expand until you become so large, so pervasive, that your company's brand name becomes a familiar part of the American lexicon. Coke, Pepsi, Microsoft, Wal-Mart, Home Depot, Lowes, and McDonald's are prime examples of giant businesses that have become market shapers. Their concern is directed not so much to customer appetites and wants as to the strategic moves of their competitors. The requirement for success is to outsmart competitors. Strategies used by this form of competitive advantage are usually bold actions (acquisitions, joint ventures, exclusive supplier relationships, new product development, new market entries, warranties or guarantees, integrated sales and IT structures), rather than incremental improvements.

One of the clearest illustrations of this market dominance strategy is Wal-Mart. Its value proposition to its customers (quality, customer service, and convenience, always at a low price) is so consistent that few, if any, competitors can match it. This strategy depends on continually growing

> *General Motors could buy Delaware if DuPont were willing to sell it.*
> —RALPH NADER[6]

market share, volume purchases, a superb supply chain, and employee relations. For firms like Wal-Mart and McDonald's, as the United States becomes saturated, growth must come from overseas.

## QUESTIONS AND COMMENTS

As you review the three differentiation strategies and the two scale strategies that we have presented as ways to stand out in relation to your competitors, some logical questions may come to mind:

- Is it better to choose only one competitive advantage strategy to pursue?

- Is there a sequence of strategies that businesses go through as they travel through their organizational life cycle?

- To be truly world class, don't businesses have to embrace all five strategies at the same time?

> *I don't know the keys to success, but the key to failure is trying to please everybody.*
> —BILL COSBY[7]

The remainder of this chapter is devoted to answering these questions.

## The "Curly Rule"

On one side of this discussion there is what we call the "Curly rule." Curly is the character played by actor Jack Palance in the movie *City Slickers*. During the course of the movie he gives advice to another character, played by Billy

> *He who chases two rabbits at the same time catches neither.*
> —ANONYMOUS

Crystal. Curly's advice is to seek to be good at one thing in life. To try to be expert at more than one thing will result (in the end) in being expert at nothing. For example, if you were to pursue the low-cost strategy at the same time you were trying to become the best at customer service, you would increase your costs. Many business leaders subscribe to the "Curly rule" with the same belief. A business wastes resources by trying to follow two masters.

## Why Not Do It All?

On the other hand, many Asia-based organizations (and a few American firms) take a very different philosophical stance. Eastern philosophy tends to be more inclusive than the competitive, individualistic, single-minded Western approach. An Eastern-style company may very well believe that product uniqueness and strong service performance at an economical price with clear target markets must be pursued in a holistic competitive strategy. Anything less than including (and improving) all considerations would be considered very shortsighted. We'll leave the answer to you. Can your organization do it all?

# ASSESSING BUSINESS STRATEGY

Using Action Tools 3 and 4, on pages 39 and 40, respectively, may clarify how the pursuit of competitive advantage is affecting you and your organization. Action Tool 3 can help you assess the extent to which CEO plans and business strategy drive change in your organization. Action Tool 4 helps you assess a specific planned change and determine if the business strategy is the source of motivation for that change as you develop your compelling story.

ACTION TOOL 3

# Business Strategy Exercise

**Directions:** Place a check mark in the box that best describes your company's business strategy. Write brief answers to questions 2–5.

1. Which competitive advantage below is most descriptive of your organization's business strategy?

**Differentiation Strategies**

☐ Provide the best customer service

☐ Build better mousetraps (product attributes)

☐ Carve out your special piece of the pie (niche strategy)

**Scale Strategies**

☐ Provide the lowest price (cost orientation)

☐ Be the 800-pound gorilla (market dominance)

2. Why has your organization chosen this strategy?

3. How many CEOs have you had in the past fifteen years?

4. How has your business strategy shifted over time?

5. Which strategy do the employees think is the best?

ACTION TOOL 4

---

## Determining the Impact of Business Strategy

**Directions:** To what extent is business strategy at the root of reasons to implement the strategic initiative for which you are responsible? Circle the percentage below that you think best answers this question. Next, check the appropriate box to indicate the main source of pressure for this change. Finally, write a few sentences to describe some of the specific details driving this change.

0%   10%   20%   30%   40%   50%   60%   70%   80%   90%   100%

### Describe the Source for Change

**Which Advantage**

☐ Customer Service      ☐ Cost Orientation
☐ Product Attributes    ☐ Market Dominance
☐ Niche Market

**What are some of the specific details of this source?**

_____

_____

_____

_____

---

# THE BOTTOM LINE

Every firm needs a sustainable business strategy. The question is, Which one (or ones)? We have presented what we believe are the five strategic options from which firms could choose. While this book is not meant to fully teach you about competitive advantage, the CEO's strategic direction usually sparks multiple changes that must be led and implemented at all levels. The more understanding of strategy a sponsor of change has—and can communicate— the more compelling the business case will be.

If your organization wants to be around in ten years, you had better develop expertise at something that creates value for your customers. It is illustrative to look at *Fortune* magazine's top ten (or fifty) this year and then go back and look at the list from thirty or fifty years ago. What happened to all those companies? They lost their competitive advantage! The search for competitive advantage is one of the sources for change in organizations.

Actually, most U.S. companies have developed fairly good skills related to anticipating potential difficulties and crafting effective strategic directions. Often, these strategies culminate in projects that attempt to put them into action. These projects are usually called "strategic initiatives" and are most often sponsored by members of the CEO's team. Strategic initiatives almost always cause significant and important change in the organization—but all too often, they fail during implementation. For example, in one study of 210 North American managers, the researchers found that 70–75 percent of major organizational change efforts fail to meet the expectations of key stakeholders.[9] Read on to see ways to avoid that sad fate.

> *Nothing focuses the mind better than the constant sight of a competitor who wants to wipe you off the map.*
> —WAYNE CALLOWAY[8]

# Identify the Internal Fitness Requirements Driving Change

*I skate to where the puck is going to be,
not where it is or where it has been.*
—WAYNE GRETZKY[1]

Change isn't driven just by external factors or the business strategy devised to meet them, as discussed in the two preceding chapters. The third and final primary source of change that we address is the desire to enhance the organization's internal fitness, to build internal capability so as to compete better.

As you explore this chapter, remember the racing metaphor we presented earlier. In the racing business, it is widely known that the real secret of achieving greater speed lies in building capability. Speed is a by-product of two factors: the capacity of the car to accelerate, turn, brake, and so on, and the skills of the driver. The more these two capacities are increased, the quicker the car and driver will be able to be. Speed is a by-product of capacity and skill![2] This same logic can be applied to other metaphors, such as running and learning to play a musical instrument. Practice. Seek advice. Build skill, and speed increases will follow.

# THE IMPORTANCE OF ORGANIZATIONAL INFRASTRUCTURE

The concept of building skill to gain speed applies to business as well. Improve the capability of the organization's infrastructure, and the organization will be able to attain greater efficiency, satisfy customers more fully, and change directions more quickly. Organizational effectiveness should not be the goal . . . organizational effectiveness is the result of improved capability.

The purpose of evaluating internal fitness is to determine the organization's ability to compete and to achieve its business strategy. Once this assessment has been made, it may reveal areas that must be changed if the organization is to remain competitive. Internal fitness, then, is the third key driver of change.

## Capabilities for Competing in the Twenty-first Century

There are many ways to think about the important organizational knowledge, skills, and abilities needed for success. The literature on organizational theory contains countless models and frameworks, all constructed to explain the various facets of infrastructure. These models vary greatly in the number of key elements identified in the organization's infrastructure. The importance of these models is that they provide a perspective, a way to think about, assess, and plan for improved organizational capability. Because we agree with the value of these perspectives, we have created our own diagnostic framework to share with you. In the remainder of this chapter, we explore what we believe are the four most significant factors contributing to internal organizational fitness: strategic leadership, customer value, people and culture, and technological infrastructure.

Table 4 gives an overview of the four internal factors and provides examples of some of the elements in each area.

### Strategic Leadership

Demonstrating strategic leadership is one of the most important capabilities for firms in the twenty-first century. Leadership and management are different concepts. Management is concerned with efficiencies—the optimum use

TABLE 4
# Internal Fitness Requirements

| Strategic Leadership | Customer Value |
|---|---|
| - Competitive analysis | - Customer requirements |
| - Mission, vision, and values | - Product and service development |
| - Goals and strategies | - Quality processes |
| - Financial management | - Lean production techniques |
| - Strategic initiatives | - Customer satisfaction feedback |
| - Resource deployment | - Supply chain management |
| - Management of change | - Benchmarking |
| - Continuous monitoring | |

| People and Culture | Technological Infrastructure |
|---|---|
| - Productivity | - Data warehousing and mining |
| - Strategic alignment | - Customer information systems |
| - Teamwork | - Management information systems |
| - Reward systems | - Equipment |
| - Creativity and innovation | - Communication systems |
| - Learning organization | - E-commerce |

of resources. Leadership is defined by effectiveness—moving in the right direction to accomplish the right goals.

Strategic leadership includes crafting a scintillating vision, identifying the correct business plan (ensuring growth and profits), and inspiring the commitment of the people.

> *Managers are people who do things right, and leaders are people who do the right things.*
> —WARREN G. BENNIS[3]

Strategic leadership requires visionary skills, a strong industry analysis, astute strategic planning, and the skillful management of resources. Many organizations are adept at identifying the strategic initiatives needed to achieve their business strategy. These initiatives typically represent the important changes that must be made for future business success. In other words, organizational leaders are fairly good at choosing among strategic alternatives. But it is not enough just to be a brilliant strategic planner. It is at least equally important to skillfully lead and manage the implementation of the changes.

## Customer Value

The second important internal capability is the ability to understand and deliver the value proposition your organization offers its customers. Once customer value is understood, the organization must then find ways to economically deliver the products and services that fulfill the proposition. Many of the skills and abilities required by the customer value proposition originate in the total quality management processes developed in the 1980s. Abilities like knowing customers' requirements, using lean production techniques, and providing efficient supply chain management all contribute to a stronger customer value proposition.

> *In every instance, we found that the best run companies stay as close to their customers as humanly possible.*
> —THOMAS J. PETERS[4]

Normally, once quality assurances are in place and customer expectations are being met, the ante for survival in your industry has been paid. But these are not normal times. Consumers and competitors seem to be continually raising the bar for price, convenience, speed, delivery, and service. This escalation of customer and competitor expectations necessitates an equally continual improvement for the organizational processes that deliver the value proposition.

## People and Culture

The third important internal capability required to compete in the twenty-first century is leading and managing the human side of the enterprise. Skillfully managing people is a capability that can differentiate a business in many different industries. For example, the service sector of our economy is highly dependent on people to deliver its value proposition. In fact, in most service industries, it is the lowest person in the hierarchy who encounters and interacts with the customers. In a bank, the customer's impressions come from the tellers. In a restaurant, the waiters, waitresses, and cooks determine the experience. On an airplane, the customer's impressions are formed by interactions with the ticket agents, baggage handlers, and flight attendants. The customers don't know who the vice president of operations is, and they don't care. That is why mega-retailers like McDonald's and Home Depot depend so heavily on their ability to attract and train large numbers of the right kind of entry-level employees to achieve their business strategy.

Managing the people and culture of the organization is critical in manufacturing firms, as well. People determine the refinement of product attributes, the product quality, and the industrial sales relationships. The organizational culture determines acceptable behavior and factors such as resistance to change.

> *You can dream, create, design, and build the most wonderful place in the world, but it requires people to make the dream a reality.*
>
> —WALT DISNEY[5]

These are the key "people and culture" skills and abilities that organizations must possess to pursue their business strategy effectively:

- Reliable recruitment, testing, and selection processes

- Appropriate training and development programming

- Meaningful, instrumental, and innovative reward systems

- Motivating and enabling job designs

- Open communication channels

- A culture of creativity, learning, and contribution

The necessity of training and developing the people and enhancing the organizational culture can be a tough sell in hard economic times. When funds are tight, the money needed for improving employee capabilities may be difficult to acquire. Additionally, managers often suffer from the misperception that employee development increases costs without directly contributing to revenue. This point of view, of course, is an illusion because human ingenuity and productivity are essentials for competitive success. And speaking of costs, what are the costs of an inadequately trained workforce? An inadequately motivated workforce? Deteriorating customer service? Defective products? Or massive resistance to a needed strategic change?

## Technological Infrastructure

The final internal capability required to compete in the twenty-first century involves having the proper equipment—automation, technology, systems, and the like. The real key to making technological choices is knowing which technologies to invest in, which technologies to pass on, and which technologies to outsource. With the rapid rate of technological advancement, obsolescence is taking place every day. Some technologies have the shelf life of cottage cheese. To keep up with this rate of advancement many organizations have standing orders with their personal computer suppliers to automatically change equipment every two to three years, or sooner.

> *If the only tool you have is a hammer, you tend to see every problem (or solution) as a nail.*
> —ABRAHAM MASLOW[6]

When you combine the increasing rate of technological change and obsolescence with the increasing costs of some technological equipment, systems, and maintenance staffs, you can easily see why this is one of the four factors for competitive success. Whether you are reaching into shallow or deep organizational pockets, knowing which technologies to invest in, which technologies to ignore, and how to stay the course to realize an adequate return on your investment is an important key to organizational technology fitness.

## Diagnosing the Infrastructure's Current Capability

Now that you have seen our four-pronged internal fitness model, what should you do? Our format may make sense to you, but how can you actually use it? You need a practical tool, a way to evaluate your organization's internal strengths and weaknesses. We have provided you with the necessary tool, the "Internal Fitness Survey" (Action Tool 5). We hope that applying the instrument will give you a much clearer idea of where changes could best support your competitive success.

The averages you generate in Action Tool 5 should allow you to do two things. First, the values provide a means to rank the four items and determine where you are weakest and strongest in terms of internal fitness. Second, look at the values overall—are the numbers high or low? In other words, is your internal fitness pretty good or pretty bad compared to levels needed for successful competition in your industry?

# THE THEORY OF OPTIMUM PROFICIENCY

You've probably heard the old expression that a chain is only as strong as its weakest link. By applying the theory of optimum proficiency to the results of your survey, you can gain even more valuable insight. We first encountered this theory at an organizational development conference.[7] It states that organizations (whole systems) can only be as productive as their weakest internal capabilities (your organization's lowest score on the questionnaire). For example:

- Your organization may lead the industry in technology—but if employees haven't been sufficiently trained, the technological strength is lost.

- Strategic leadership may be your organization's competitive strength—but if it is being diluted by low customer value, your leadership strength is lost.

- Your organization may be excellent in creating customer value—but if it doesn't have the resources to support it technologically, your customer value strength is lost.

Optimum proficiency suggests that you spend your change resources on improving your internal fitness in your weakest areas (lowest fitness score). In fact, the organization will more fully realize the strengths in the other three areas as the greatest weakness is shored up.

# ASSESSING INTERNAL FITNESS

Action Tool 6 can assess a specific planned change and determine if an internal weakness is the source of motivation for the change.

ACTION TOOL 5

# Internal Fitness Survey

**Directions:** Rate each question according to your perception of your organization.

**Rating Key**
**1** = Strongly disagree
**2** = Disagree
**3** = Neutral
**4** = Agree
**5** = Strongly agree
**6** = Not applicable

____ 1. Our organization periodically analyzes our competition's strengths and weaknesses and consciously assesses our position in the industry.

____ 2. We know our customers' requirements for service and product design, quality standards, and pricing.

____ 3. By any measurement one might use, our organization would prove to have highly efficient and productive operations.

____ 4. Our organization is ahead of the curve when it comes to data warehousing and being able to mine (access and extract value from) that information.

____ 5. The mission, vision, and values of our organization are clear and provide exciting and challenging direction.

____ 6. Service and product design and development is achieved through up-to-date computer-assisted equipment and tools (hardware and software).

____ 7. All our employees know how their jobs contribute to the company's goals and strategies.

____ 8. Our customer information systems enable us to handle 95 percent of customer inquiries on the first call and without transfer.

____ 9. I am confident our company's strategies and game plans will successfully achieve our strategic goals.

____ 10. We use appropriate quality assurance strategies to ensure zero defect and service reliability without rework.

____ 11. Cooperation and teamwork support our organization's ability to be cost-effective and satisfy our customers.

ACTION TOOL 5 (cont'd)

___ 12. Managers in our organization get excellent reports and information to run their business.

___ 13. We have the necessary performance measurements to get meaningful feedback so that management can adjust as necessary.

___ 14. We use the latest lean production techniques to assure cost efficiency (for example, pull manufacturing, just-in-time inventory, work cells, focused factories, and so on).

___ 15. Rewards and recognition are clearly linked to the accomplishment of our vision, mission, and goals.

___ 16. We have the equipment and service systems necessary to be competitive in our industry.

___ 17. We focus our attention on a few major strategic initiatives to avoid diluting our resources.

___ 18. We have long-term service level agreements with our key suppliers.

___ 19. We encourage creativity for effective problem solving.

___ 20. We have the systems in our organization to efficiently and quickly communicate internally.

___ 21. Our company's resources are allocated based on our strategic goals.

___ 22. We maintain performance measurements that are benchmarked to our competition's performance levels.

___ 23. Our organization often conducts debriefing sessions or postmortems while implementing strategic changes and afterward in order to learn important leadership lessons.

___ 24. Our organization is ahead of the curve in making effective use of e-commerce opportunities.

___ 25. Our utilization of managing change techniques has led to an excellent track record for implementation.

___ 26. We have very effective supply chain management techniques.

___ 27. Our organization is very good at monitoring customers, competition, technological developments, and government regulation on an ongoing basis.

ACTION TOOL 5 (cont'd)

## Internal Fitness Survey Summary

**Directions:** Place the values you gave for the questions on the "Internal Fitness Survey" in the spaces below and calculate the average for each box.

**Strategic Leadership**
1. Competitive analysis _____
5. Mission, vision,
   and values _____
9. Goals and strategies _____
13. Financial management _____
17. Strategic initiatives _____
21. Resource deployment _____
25. Management of change _____
27. Continuous monitoring _____
**Average** _____

**Customer Value**
2. Customer requirements _____
6. Product and service
   development _____
10. Quality production
   processes _____
14. Lean production techniques _____
18. Supplier relationships _____
22. Benchmarking _____
26. Supply chain management _____
**Average** _____

**People and Culture**
3. Productivity _____
7. Strategic alignment _____
11. Teamwork _____
15. Reward systems _____
19. Creativity and innovation _____
23. Learning organization _____
**Average** _____

**Technological Infrastructure**
4. Data warehousing
   and mining _____
8. Customer information
   systems _____
12. Management information
   systems _____
16. Equipment _____
20. Communication systems _____
24. E-commerce _____
**Average** _____

ACTION TOOL 6

## Determining the Impact of Internal Fitness

**Directions:** To what extent is internal fitness the reason to implement the strategic initiative for which you are responsible? To answer this question, circle the percentage below that seems most accurate. Next, check the box that indicates the main source of pressure for this change. Finally, write a few sentences to describe some of the specific details driving this change.

0%   10%   20%   30%   40%   50%   60%   70%   80%   90%   100%

### Describe the Source for Change

**Which capability?**

☐ Strategic Leadership        ☐ Technological Infrastructure

☐ Customer Value              ☐ People and Culture

**What are some of the specific details of this source?**

_____

_____

_____

_____

# THE BOTTOM LINE

You may be asking yourself, So what? Why go to all this trouble? For example, you may decide to make your products smaller and lighter. Assume that your CEO has empirically reasoned that smaller and lighter will add 5 percent market share. Further, assume that this opportunity will catch your competition by surprise. Why bother going through all the analyses we have suggested? Who cares about the cause of the change if the change must be implemented?

The answer is that the employees who must embrace the change and successfully implement it . . . care! Knowing that an external threat is calling for the company's reaction and response . . . matters. Knowing that the CEO has a plan that will set this company apart from its competitors . . . matters. Knowing that an infrastructure upgrade is needed to fully execute the company's business strategy . . . matters. It is in the clear explanation of why the organization must change, and why it must make this particular change, that the commitment and motivation of the affected workforce begins. A clear explanation of the need for change and the expected benefits to be realized appeals to all the participants' sense of logic, need to know, and wish for inclusion in the process. An illustration of the three primary drivers (external pressure, business strategy, internal capability) is provided in Figure 2. This illustration summarizes the sources discussed in Chapters 2, 3, and 4.

A thorough analysis provides leaders and followers alike with

- An understanding of the need for change

- An explanation of the motivation for change

- The benefits of changing

- The costs of not changing

- What must be done to successfully implement the change

This clear, rational, complete analysis conveys a far more compelling truth than any number of fiery "we have to make this change to survive—if we don't do it, we are all doomed" statements. People who must follow and implement the change will always respond better to the simple truth than to a long list of rationalizations.

FIGURE 2
## Sources of Organizational Change

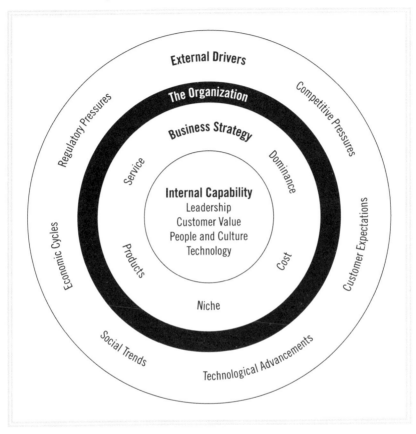

# Communicate a Compelling Change Story

*The mind is like the stomach. It is not how much you
put into it that counts, but how much it digests.*
—ALBERT JAY NOCK[1]

So far, you've identified the sources of the pressures for change. You have
begun to build a systematic understanding of why the organization must
make the change. Now it's time for the all-important next step—articulating
and clearly communicating the business case for change. This event, typically
the official launch of the change, is absolutely critical to begin to garner
employee buy-in and to grease the wheels for the successful implementation
of the change—on time, on target, on budget! The employees directly affected
by the change (and from whom you want belief in the change) are waiting,
watching, and wondering.

Your explanation of why their company is changing is your first real
opportunity to anticipate employees' concerns and begin to chip away at individual resistance to change. (We get back to individual resistance in more
detail in Chapter 8.)

# ARTICULATING THE BUSINESS CASE FOR CHANGE

Your first critical communication task is to organize your material in a way that anticipates employees' expectations, questions, and concerns. Structure your information in the following order:

1. Present the background, the setting, the situation in which you and your people find yourselves (revisit Chapters 2, 3, and 4).

2. Explain what the pressures for change are and where they are originating.

3. Illustrate why change is needed.

4. Demonstrate what is likely to happen if the company doesn't change.

5. Show why this change is the best choice out of all the possibilities.

6. Describe all the realistic potential benefits from successfully implementing the change.

7. Show the fact-based costs and benefits of pursuing the change.

8. Indicate how this change will roll out—the next steps.

9. Be prepared to answer any and all questions regarding the change.

10. Close by explaining the process that you will use to allow objections and concerns to be heard throughout the implementation process.

# CRAFTING A COMPELLING PRESENTATION OF THE CHANGE STORY

Sharing the explanation of the change with the employees should be a continuous process, not a one-time event. However, whether it is the initial memo regarding the projected change, the communication announcing the formal meeting where the change will be addressed and who is invited, or the actual formal presentation (with a question-and-answer session), all effective communications on the change should follow a similar pattern and logic. Since the formal presentation designed to communicate the change story is probably the single most important event, the remainder of this chapter focuses on designing and executing an effective presentation. Just keep in mind that the material in this chapter applies to any and all of your communications regarding the change.

The presentation skills of managers vary a great deal. How do you, depending on your skill level, go about creating a compelling presentation of the change story? In this chapter, we introduce a comprehensive communication process that, if followed, should improve your chances of getting buy-in for the change.

## What Makes a Presentation Compelling?

Your change story should honestly convince the employees that the organizational and personal benefits of the change far outweigh the costs. You must answer the one question guaranteed to occur to everyone you need to reach: "What's in it for me?"

In our experience, we have found four general action steps that can accomplish effective communication of the need for change:

> *Surely, whoever speaks to me in the right voice, him or her I shall follow.*
> —WALT WHITMAN[2]

1. Determine your goals for the communication.

2. Work through the business communication process.

3. Check the quality of your communication.

4. View your final presentation from the employees' perspective.

We discuss each one further to help you create the most effective communication possible.

## Action Step 1: Determine Your Goals for the Communication

Get straight about why you are communicating. Different reasons demand different styles, formats, and language. You want to communicate in the right way, at the right time, to the right folks. What do you want the result of your presentation to be? (The check boxes in front of the following components enable you to keep track of where your message is strong and where it needs work.) Consider the four sets of questions to determine your primary aim:

☐ **Educate the employees?** Do you want to explain, teach, inform, or coach the employees regarding certain aspects of the change? Do you want to share information regarding the change? Do you want to make the employees more aware of aspects of the change?

☐ **Energize the employees?** Is your goal to stimulate thought? Do you want to motivate the employees to take some action?

☐ **Learn from the employees?** Do you want to have a dialogue with the employees to learn about their ideas, thoughts, concerns, and objections? Do you intend to ask for employee input? Is your goal to discover what is on the employees' minds?

☐ **Sell the change to the employees?** Are you trying to persuade the employees to view the change as desirable? Do you want to convince the employees to accept and back the change?

Finally, how will you know if you have achieved your purpose? Do you have the proper feedback mechanisms in place to tell you?

## Action Step 2: Work Through the Business Communication Process

Now that you know your goals, how do you get there? Treat the communication like any other business process: develop a plan, prepare thoroughly, package it well, and promote it tastefully.

### Develop a Plan

Communicating a strategic initiative is very complex, so you must have a plan. What do you need to know about your audience? What are the basics of your message? How should you get your main points across? What medium will best achieve your purpose and convey your thoughts to this audience? What excites you about the prospect? (If the change itself doesn't excite you, how will it excite others?) How might you be able to create enthusiasm regarding the possibilities? How would a successful change help you? How might it help someone else or the entire organization? What opportunities might emerge if this change is performed superbly? The more passionate you are about the change, the more effort you will exert, and the more persuasive the communication will become.

## Prepare Thoroughly

To do anything well, you must prepare and practice. Being prepared is vital to successful implementation of the change. The sooner you start to prepare, the more time you allow yourself for thinking and the likelier you are to discover the ideal approach.

Sooner or later, you need to start writing. It's really tough to react to a blank screen or page. Write anything. Scribble down words, thoughts, or ideas as you get them. Draw something that comes to mind. Continue to brainstorm in spite of distractions, opposition, setbacks, obstacles, or disappointments. Persist. Be a hungry dog with a bone! Look at it this way—preparation is not wasting time or spending time; it is investing time.

## Package It Well

Dress your presentation for success! No matter how good your message is, if it gets wrapped in the wrong package, it will be rejected. Perfecting, polishing, and packaging the change message for different groups of employees is not the most exciting task, but it is critical. Try to view it from the perspective of the employees. What can you say to encourage buy-in? How much structure should you provide? Is audience involvement appropriate or not? Keep asking yourself, What would make this change story easier for the employees to understand and accept?

Craft your communication to please your audience. What about change interests them? What style would be most appropriate? How long should the presentation be? What format should you use? Why not create a powerful, meaningful, and perhaps even catchy title or subject line? Your goal is to be heard and believed. As Ben Franklin said, "Eat to please yourself, but dress to please others."

## Promote It Tastefully

It pays to promote your communication. Why not place reminders in convenient places? Remember, you are in competition with lots of other priorities. Should you share what you are doing with other people? If you don't promote your change, you'll know what you're doing, but nobody else will.

# Action Step 3: Check the Quality of Your Communication

Your change story must be a total quality communication. Your message should be clear, compelling, correct, and crisp.

Use the check boxes to make sure your message is

☐ **Clear.** In communicating strategic initiatives, clarity is job number one. Fuzzy, confusing, "guess what I'm thinking" messages invite misinterpretations. "Communication by mind-reading" is frustrating for the audience and dangerous for the sender. Tell people everything they may want to know, and tell it in the clearest, most direct way. It's often useful to have someone else edit the message for clarity; you know what you mean, but everyone else will perceive it in his or her own way.

☐ **Compelling.** Even if your change message is clear, you won't get buy-in unless it is compelling. The content and the delivery must be appealing to the audience. Choose the content that will be most enticing to them. Develop messages that are visually attractive, balanced, varied, and alluring. Use graphic devices like boldface type, underlining key words or phrases, capitalized headings, graphics, pictures, and bullets sparingly but effectively.

☐ **Correct.** Your message must be technically correct, grammatically correct, and correctly spelled or you will be perceived as unprofessional, uneducated, careless, or even worse—as not caring enough about the message to correct the mistakes.

☐ **Complete.** To be correct, your content must also be complete. Touch all the bases; fill all the holes! Just provide all of what the employees will need. Be thorough, but don't try to stuff fifteen pounds into a five-pound bag! What should you include? What should you omit? Use common sense and your understanding of the employees to decide. Try to include "just the right amount" of depth and breadth for that group of employees. Use the leftover stuff as backup, in case you get questions pertaining to it.

Before you begin, decide on the appropriate level of language to use. As you revise and edit your communication, search for any words that are not true to the level of language you chose. Use the same person, tense, and style throughout the message. Make sure that your headings and any lists use parallel phrases or words. For example, begin every bulleted item in a list with the same part of speech, whether it's a noun, verb, adverb, or adjective.

Crafting error-free business communications won't necessarily grab your audience, but it will keep the employees from turning off your message before it has a chance to influence them.

☐ **Crisp.** As long as the critical information is present, shorter is better. Employees appreciate brevity. Check your message. Is it succinct? Do you need to tighten up your slides? Do you need a larger font? Is your format incisive? Go back through your presentation and eliminate any excess words or extraneous ideas. What is the bottom line here?

## Action Step 4: View Your Final Presentation from the Employees' Perspective

OK! Now that you have chosen your goals, carried out the stages of the business process, and checked the quality of your communication, you need to take one last step. Consider your audience again. If you don't view your final presentation from the employees' perspective, you will probably miss something important.

Your employees are always receiving tons of competing messages. To get and keep your audience's attention, your change story must be enthusiastic, personalized, short, and simple. Is your message

☐ **Enthusiastic?** If you aren't excited about the change initiative, why should the audience care? Are you enthused by the possibilities? Are you passionate regarding the launch of the change? Have you hooked the audience into sharing some of your exhilaration?

☐ **Personalized?** What's in this change initiative for the audience? How will they perceive the possible personal gains and losses in this change? People selectively pay attention to what they think will benefit them. The audience will have difficulty determining whether the change presentation has anything for them unless you design the communication to be personal, attractive, and delivered in their language. Have you helped the employees see the initiative's importance to them and its urgency to the organization?

☐ **Short?** When was the last time you saw a great presentation that was too short? The longer a communication, the less likely people will stay tuned to that channel. Long, clumsy, vague communications get little respect. Get to the point!

☐ **Simple?** When in doubt, follow Stuart Chase's advice—Keep it simple, stupid, or the readers will KISS it off. Most humans are, by nature, "mental misers." The more cluttered the message is, the more we tune out! Make sure your major points are prominent and easy to follow!

# DELIVERING THE CHANGE MESSAGE

OK! So you've expertly built your PowerPoint presentation for the change. Your slides are crafted. You are ready to go. Or are you? The science (content) has been completed. Now comes the all-important art (style) of presenting.

## Pick the Right Voice!

The choice of the presenter is a crucial one. Who is the best person to deliver this change message? Who has the most credibility? Who commands the most respect on this topic? Who will the employees believe? Who will be the sponsor now and during implementation? Make this choice carefully. Choose the best person for this change. We proceed on the assumption that you're making the presentation yourself, but the comments apply equally to another champion if you decide to choose one.

> *What people say behind your back is your standing in the community.*
> —ED HOWE[3]

## Get Pumped Up!

Telling a great change story starts with the speaker's motivation (believing in the importance of the message). Next, stimulate the employees into believing you (by modeling your faith in the change).

Many managers suffer from varying degrees of anxiety when they must speak in public. Some fear possible ridicule, embarrassment, failure, or inadequacy. "Lights! Camera! Action!" Some managers, when they get up to give a crucial talk, can see their life flashing in front of them. With pounding heart and sweaty hands, they want to shout, "Oh my, what have I gotten myself into? Why me, Lord?" Welcome to corporate theater!

> *The mind is a wonderful thing. It starts working the minute you're born and never stops until you get up to speak in public.*
> —JACOB M. BRAUDE[4]

Take a deep breath! Try to relax. You're ready. You've done your homework. You now know more about this change than anyone else. You've applied the system suggested in this chapter. Try to adopt this perspective—your objective is not to give a perfect talk. Your objective is to satisfy the employees' needs. What you do need, however, is conviction. If you show excitement and passion for the change, the employees may conclude that you have something worthwhile to share. Similarly, a lack of enthusiasm can be interpreted as a lack of commitment to this change. Enthusiasm can wash away many presentation sins.

Your research should have led you to truly believe in the value of this change. Why not tell the audience why this change is important to you and to them. Share your insights and excitement!

## You Only Get One Chance for a First Impression

Authors differ on what part of a presentation they believe is most significant. We believe the most crucial part is the opening. The beginning comments of a presentation are vital to capturing the employees' interest and setting the stage for what will follow. In today's world of channel-surfers and overflowing plates, you need an opening that grabs the employees quickly. Here are some possibilities to consider for a successful opening.[6]

> *Be the change you want to see in the world.*
> —MOHANDAS K. GANDHI[5]

- **Dive right in.** If this organizational change is obviously important to everyone, just clearly state the purpose, goal, and importance.

- **Make people laugh.** Depending on your personality and facility with humor, you could decide to use a tasteful joke, an amusing picture, a curious model, or a funny slide depicting how hard change can be on everyone.

- **Ask a penetrating rhetorical question.** For example, "How has our industry changed in the past twenty years? Look at this chart. . . ."

- **State a startling fact regarding change.** For example: "Someone has suggested that more information has been generated in the past twenty years than in the entire history of our planet up to that point!"

- **Lead off with a short video on change.** For example: "Who Moved My Cheese?"

- **Use a quotation about change.** For example: "The suicide bomber, embarking on his forty-ninth mission, is involved in the change, but not committed."

- **Use an anecdote.** For example: "Yesterday, I was waiting for a phone call from one of our suppliers and it happened again."

- **Appeal to the audience's self-interest.** For example: "Each of you will benefit from these upcoming changes in three ways. Here's how:"

- **Use an ice-breaker.** For example: "How many of you are here because you just love change? How many of you are here because you were told to be here? That's OK. Me too!"

- **Establish your credibility.** For example: "I have been managing change in this industry for thirty years!"

Whatever approach you take, memorize your opening remarks and "say it like you mean it!"

## The Meat Is in the Middle

The body of your presentation is the content, the meat—the change story (business case) you have developed to share with the audience. Focus on three or four goals. Balance the big picture and the details. Provide a few applications and implications. Give enough of a glimpse of how the change will roll out that implementation is believable.

## End with a Bang

The second most important part of your presentation is the ending. Far too many presentations end with a whimper ("Well, I don't have anything else to say, so I guess that's about it. . . .") instead of a bang ("So remember, this change is going to save the company $62 million a year without the loss of a single job!") Write, edit, and revise your ending. Memorize your closing remarks! Say them with conviction. End with a bang!

## Watch Your Body Language

The greatest words can be killed by inconsistent body language. People believe what they see for themselves, and they're watching you—not just listening. In one famous study, for example, Dr. Albert Mehrabian discovered that in an interpersonal exchange, 55 percent of the content was transmitted by facial expressions and body posture, 38 percent was derived from inflexion and tone of voice, and words accounted for only 7 percent of the meaning received.[7] In other words, most of the meaning transferred (93 percent) was *not* in the words. Isn't that finding bizarre? Ninety-three percent! Maybe the study is off a little and the percentage is really only 80 percent. Yikes! That's still incredible. The power of nonverbal communication is astounding. Bear this surprising study in mind. When you give that presentation, don't send mixed messages. Watch your body language, facial expression, inflection, and tone of voice!

## TRACKING YOUR PRESENTATION

Table 5 provides an overview of this chapter and allows a quick check on your progress and what remains to be done.[8] Action Tool 7 gives you a framework for the final step in preparing your change presentation.

TABLE 5

| Articulating and Communicating a Compelling Change Story | | | |
|---|---|---|---|
| **Action Step 1** | **Action Step 2** | **Action Step 3** | **Action Step 4** |
| Determine your goals! | Work through the business process! | Check the quality! | View from the employees' perspective! |
| ▪ Educate<br>▪ Energize<br>▪ Learn<br>▪ Sell | ▪ Develop a plan<br>▪ Prepare thoroughly<br>▪ Package it well<br>▪ Promote it tastefully | ▪ Clear<br>▪ Compelling<br>▪ Correct<br>▪ Crisp | ▪ Enthusiastic<br>▪ Personalized<br>▪ Short<br>▪ Simple |

ACTION TOOL 7

---

# Reviewing Your Change Story

**Directions:** Answer questions 1–5 to ensure the success of your presentation.

1. Have you clearly identified the goal for your change presentation?

   ☐ Educate?

   ☐ Energize?

   ☐ Learn?

   ☐ Sell?

2. Take a long, hard look at your change presentation. Think about the attributes of a quality communication, the business process you need to perform, and the audience's perspective. Now, rank the product and process attributes of your change presentation on a scale of 1–4, with 1 representing what you have done best and 4 representing what you have done worst. Then rank the presentation from the employees' perspective on the same 1–4 scale.

| Quality Presentation Attributes | Quality Product Process | Employees' Perspective |
|---|---|---|
| ___ Clear | ___ Plan | ___ Enthusiastic |
| ___ Compelling | ___ Prepare | ___ Personalized |
| ___ Correct | ___ Package | ___ Short |
| ___ Crisp | ___ Promote | ___ Simple |

ACTION TOOL 7 (cont'd)

3. Select your worst item in each category and develop an action plan to turn this weakness into a strength.

   Quality Product Attribute Weakness:

   _____

   Plan of Action (three improvements you will make):

   _____

   _____

   _____

   Quality Product Process Weakness:

   _____

   Plan of Action (three improvements you will make):

   _____

   _____

   _____

   Employees' Perspective Weakness:

   _____

   Plan of Action (three improvements you will make):

   _____

   _____

   _____

ACTION TOOL 7 (cont'd)

---

**4.** Have you carefully articulated and memorized your opening remarks?_____
What will you say?

_____

_____

_____

**5.** Have you carefully articulated and memorized your closing remarks?_____
What will you say?

_____

_____

_____

---

# THE BOTTOM LINE

Flawless business communications don't just happen. Total quality communications are purposeful, well planned, free of defects, and audience oriented. Carefully honing your presentation on change is critical. Delivering your change message effectively is paramount. You need both substance *and* style!

This chapter has presented our own spin on the process of creating a compelling presentation on a change initiative. The principles apply to any communication involving the change, from e-mail to posters to formal meetings. Table 5 summarized the advice given in this chapter. Why not make some copies of it? Paste it on your wall, and review it to double-check any communication regarding the change—before you send it or say it.

# 2

# ANTICIPATE IMPLEMENTATION ISSUES

As the voice whispered in *Field of Dreams,* "If you build it, they will come." If you build the case for change carefully and tell the change story well, the employees will momentarily suspend, or at least question, their disbelief.

Now it's time to implement and sustain the change. Successfully implementing organizational change (on time, on target, and on budget) is a more mundane, pedantic, and tricky—but crucial—process that hinges on management's ability to

- Anticipate the likely roadblocks

- Take preemptive action to defuse the objections

- Develop strategies to reduce potential barriers

## ENABLING AND DISABLING FORCES

With any organizational change, there are always favorable (enabling) forces working in support of the change and unfavorable (disabling) forces operating to derail the change. Enabling forces might include elements such as these:

- A good fit between the proposed change and the existing organizational culture

- Clearly beneficial outcomes for individual participants

- A credible sponsor and strong project team leader

- A cross-functional, committed project team

- An ample budget for staffing, supplies, and support

The disabling forces at work might include elements such as these:

- Conflict with what the organizational culture supports

- Personal fears, threats, and insecurities

- Inadequate sponsorship

- Turf battles and functional silos

- Inadequate budget for staffing, supplies, and support

In this battle between the enabling forces and the disabling forces, your implementation objective is to reach what Malcolm Gladwell calls "the tipping point."[1] You want to implement skillfully so as to tip the scales, to achieve that moment of critical mass where

- The weight (the balance of power) begins to tilt, tip, shift in favor of the change

- The change then slowly builds momentum and mass as it rolls downhill, gathering speed and mass

- The change begins to move forward, taking on a life of its own—the change is able to sustain itself

## ANTICIPATIVE CORRECTIONS

To enhance the enabling forces and hold the disabling forces at bay, you must be able to practice *anticipative corrections* (intercepting problems before they occur and taking preventive action) rather than *reactive corrections*, (rectifying problems after they occur—damage control). Anticipative corrections include

- Recognizing the potential barriers prior to implementation

- Prioritizing the potential obstacles in terms of the level of resistance you are likely to encounter

- Devising creative strategies to short-circuit the resistance prior to implementation

In our observations, one of the most significant differences between effective change leaders and less mature change leaders is their ability to foresee problems. Really good change managers know their people and business so well that they are able to stay ahead of the impending derailments. They take preventive action before the trouble has a chance to start. They seem to intuitively know when they are headed for a derailment, and they act to keep it from happening.

You can witness this phenomenon with the truly great sports stars. Pittsburgh Penguins star Mario Lemieux will, at crucial moments, move to a place on the ice where the hockey puck will soon be. Former Pittsburgh Steelers wide receiver Lynn Swann

> *Today you must be in the right place before the right time.*
> —ROSABETH MOSS KANTER

would move toward the flight of a pass from quarterback Terry Bradshaw before he turned his head to see the ball. Race car driver Mario Andretti would begin turning the steering wheel to regain traction before the skid took place. The great ones all seem to have this ability to anticipate, this eerie intuition that allows them to know what is going to happen next.

In contrast, the inexperienced and perhaps less talented change manager probably assumes that these anticipative actions are the result of extremely skilled reactions. No sponsor can plan for all circumstances and events. Quick reactions are part of managing change, but anticipation is the real art. Extinguishing fires can be a great adrenaline rush, so great that stimulus junkies sometimes even create crises so that they can solve them and look heroic, but truly successful change management looks calm and easy instead.

# WHAT LIES AHEAD

Part Two of this book begins by examining the potential roadblocks to successful implementation to help you build the ability and capacity to anticipate and stay ahead of derailments. The chapters on successful implementation that follow support more preventive action and help minimize the chances for surprise or derailment.

More specifically, Chapter 6 introduces the resistance factors by explaining three very distinct types of changes. It suggests some managerial implications of launching and implementing each type of change. While the barriers to implementation are common across all changes, the order and importance of the barriers shift with different types of change.

The remaining chapters (7–11) explore the five most common roadblocks (organizational culture, individual resistance, inadequate sponsorship, silo mentalities, and resource constraints) and suggest ways to reduce or overcome these obstacles. We've arranged these five chapters according to our view of the importance of each barrier as a potential obstacle across all types and degrees of change.

Part Two will help you identify the roadblocks, anticipate corrections, and smooth the way for sustaining change.

# Recognize Different Types of Change

*If you don't know where you're going,*
*you'll probably end up somewhere else."*
—DAVID CAMPBELL[1]

Jeez! Just when you thought . . .

- It was safe to go back into the water!

- You had all the bases covered!

- You had your ducks lined up in a row!

- You had your stuff together!

We're going to ask you to be analytical again and answer one more important question: What type of change are you launching? When it comes to organizational change, one size does not fit all. Just as changing a flat tire on your car is distinct from buying a new DVD player at a great price, which is unlike changing your career, the species of change matters. This chapter is designed to help you understand the kind of change you are launching and the ramifications of the effort.

Organizational changes can vary from continuous improvements to reorganizations to strategy redirections to new markets to acquisitions or mergers to cultural shifts.

To help you differentiate changes, we identify and describe three very distinct types of organizational change in this chapter, each of which has a number of characteristic features:[2]

- Each type is accompanied by a distinctive level of needed involvement.

- Each type is affected by distinctive obstacles.

- Each type is bound by a distinctive time frame.

- Each type is disruptive to different functions to varying degrees.

- Each type is divergent in size and scope.

- Each type is driven by a distinctive source.

- Each type is led and managed in disparate ways for successful implementation.

- Each type is prone to different kinds of problems.

- Each type is sponsored distinctively.

- Each type is subject to different levels of resistance.

We refer to these three types of change as developmental, opportunistic, and transformational.

# DEVELOPMENTAL CHANGE

Developmental change is, by nature, incremental and unending. It is synonymous with gradual, careful, constant growth, with progress and evolution.

> *We are what we repeatedly do. Excellence, then, is not an act, but a habit.*
> —ARISTOTLE[3]

The possibilities for advancement are lengthy and infinite. The goal (never reached) is to grow into a more complete, more correct, more desirable, more nearly perfect state. "Getting the bugs out" never really ends. The quest for organizational maturity is an admirable journey. Realistically, all organizations are in various stages of improvement or decline. Organizations evolve over time and in context. The pursuit of excellence has no finish line.

Developmental changes can range from small, gradual advances in productivity or incremental cost reductions (such as those found in the total quality and continuous improvement processes) to more significant and longer-term advancements (such as improving customer value or investing more in executive development). Developmental changes can lead to the achievement of a new plateau (such as the move from a regional to a national business).

Incremental changes can provide small surprises, but they occur pretty much as expected. You can't necessarily name the day and hour that the next small breakthrough will occur, but you generally know what the next step is. If you work at it diligently, it will materialize within a predictable period of time. For example, you may be working on moving your defect rate from 2 percent to 1 percent. With effort and energy, you can make it happen. Likewise, you can predict with reasonable confidence that as your organization grows and succeeds (usually over decades), it will naturally evolve through the stages of the life cycle (birth, youth, midlife, maturity, and decline).[4] The problem with developmental change is that the never-ending nature of the pursuit of excellence can grind down the will, sap the energy, numb the spirit, and become ho-hum. Developmental change takes a special kind of patient bulldog to hang on and see it through.

Developmental change is driven by the quest to upgrade the internal organizational environment in order to be more competitive.

## OPPORTUNISTIC CHANGE

When opportunity knocks, will your company be home? *Opportunity* is a favorable or advantageous combination of circumstances. As changes go, the opportunistic variety tend to occur most quickly. For example, someone spots a strategic possibility —the strategic window is temporarily open, and the organization either takes immediate advantage or decides to pass.

> *The greatest risk of all is to do nothing.*
> —ROBERT GOIZUETA[5]

Some opportunistic changes are partially planned in the sense that the organization is searching, scanning, and therefore alert to the good fortune its people may spot. Also, the opportunity is recognized to be congruent with a conscious vision and strategy—it fits the organization's direction and targets. Other fortuitous changes are unplanned —someone merely sizes up a lucky event and seizes the opening. Examples might include a new market opening up unexpectedly or a leading competitor experiencing supply or labor problems.

Some opportunities are more obvious than others. On the more subtle side, every day, some industries are reshaped by patterns of change that have the potential to shift profits, power, and competitive balance.[6] For example, GE identified the emerging pattern as "solutions" (products *and* services). Microsoft and Nucor perceived the pattern (opportunity) to be "de-integration" (discarding costly pieces of the value chain). For Coca-Cola, the opportunity was "re-integration" (adding bottling and distribution). However, seeing the pattern and recognizing the opportunity it provides are scarce skills. When you find these skills anywhere in your organization, treasure them, nurture them!

Opportunistic changes tend to be driven by events (pressures) in the external environment. Keep your environmental scanning gear handy. Get your antenna up! Just think how many people saw an apple fall before Sir Isaac Newton observed one and asked why apples fell.

# TRANSFORMATIONAL CHANGE

To *transform* something means to markedly change its form, function, nature, or condition. Transformational changes are large (organization-wide), long term (several years), complete, radical alterations. Although transformational change is planned in the sense that someone decides that the organization needs to be converted, it does not always play out in predictable ways. This metamorphosis involves an emergence to a new, different state, unknown until it actually occurs and takes shape (like a caterpillar changing into a butterfly).

> *Every act of creation is first of all an act of destruction.*
> —**PABLO PICASSO**[7]

Leading a transformation requires a recognition of the need for huge modifications, the creation of a vision to drive and guide the change, and a plan to execute the change effectively. With radical changes, the journey and outcome are often unpredictable. When you begin to totally reinvent an organization, you cannot be sure exactly where the pilgrimage will take you, and unexpected events happen along the way. For example, as you integrate electronic technology into your company culture, you might inadvertently turn e-mail into an informal grapevine, disseminating rumors throughout the organization. Additionally, as Picasso says, with every radical creation, some disassembly (destruction) is required.

Transformational change does not happen evenly or cleanly. Massive change, change of the size and scope called for here, stirs up and shakes up a bunch of interdependent activities. Change of this scale disrupts every nook and cranny in the firm. Work patterns are altered, people need training, systems must be redesigned. With all this apparent chaos, the change, if not led and managed expertly, can easily lose momentum and direction.

Transformational changes are usually driven by the CEO's vision and the competitive environment. Consequently, the stability of the organizational leadership contributes to the level of resistance to change. Every time an organization replaces its CEO, a new leader arrives who puts a new stamp on the organization—a new strategic direction. The more often you change CEOs, the greater the probability that the employees will get change-sick (a form of motion sickness) from the yo-yo-ing. Changing directions frequently also leads people to fall back on the all-purpose insight "This, too, shall pass!"

We wish you the joy of stable, visionary leadership. Employees are already suffering enough "change initiative fatigue" from all the tools and fads adopted and discarded lately. Speaking of which, whatever happened to Total Quality Management (TQM)? Empowering Employees (EE)? Business Process Redesign (BPR)? Were they downsized? Right-sized? Blindsided? Or did they fall into the black hole of change? Maybe there is a lesson about managing change here. Labeling changes has an upside and a downside. Giving something a name helps people focus on it and reinforce it. But be careful. It seems that the minute a change receives an acronym, it begins to fade.

> *You can't step into the same river twice.*
> —HERACLITUS[8]

Table 6 supplies a summary of the types of change, with some examples and the issues for each kind of change. Table 7 presents the main characteristics of and some examples of appropriate management practices for each type of change.

TABLE 6

## Types of Change, Examples, and Issues

| Type | Typical Source | Examples | Issues |
|---|---|---|---|
| Developmental Change | Desire to enhance internal fitness | ▪ Product improvements<br>▪ Process improvements<br>▪ Technology and systems improvements<br>▪ Human systems improvements<br>▪ Human capital improvements<br>▪ Evolution from national to multinational firm | ▪ Cultural roadblocks<br>▪ Planned improvement of capability<br>▪ High, selective involvement |
| Opportunistic Change | Response to external drivers | ▪ New product innovations<br>▪ New and emergent markets<br>▪ Competitive shifts<br>▪ Mergers and acquisitions<br>▪ New industries | ▪ Cultural roadblocks<br>▪ Speed versus premature entry<br>▪ Low involvement |
| Transformational Change | Desire to gain competitive advantage | ▪ Leadership change<br>▪ Regulation and deregulation<br>▪ Large acquisition<br>▪ Reorganization | ▪ Cultural roadblocks<br>▪ Ambiguity and sustaining momentum<br>▪ Total involvement |

Now complete Action Tool 8. Specifically write out the change you are launching. Carefully naming and describing the change is not easy to do well, but it's worth doing, as clarity here will make everything else much easier. Then follow the directions to complete the other three steps of the exercise.

TABLE 7
# Change Characteristics and Supportive Practices

| Characteristics of Type | Type of Change | | |
|---|---|---|---|
| | Developmental | Opportunistic | Transformational |
| **Source** | ▪ Internal fitness | ▪ External drivers | ▪ Competitive advantage |
| **Time Frame** | ▪ Evolutionary (firm life cycle) | ▪ Short window of opportunity | ▪ Revolutionary (intermediate, 3–10 years) |
| **Predictability** | ▪ Mostly planned (incremental) | ▪ Unexpected (size up and seize) | ▪ Organic (partly planned and partly unexpected) |
| **Involvement** | ▪ High, selective involvement | ▪ Low involvement | ▪ Total involvement |
| **Management Practices, Programs, Strategies, and Techniques** | ▪ Continuous feedback<br>▪ Quality teams<br>▪ Reward and recognition systems<br>▪ Strong project management<br>▪ Training and development | ▪ Capacity to work under pressure<br>▪ Environmental scanning process<br>▪ Nimble opportunity assessment processes and due diligence<br>▪ Quick advance preparation<br>▪ Strong negotiation skills | ▪ Compelling vision for the future<br>▪ Emerging reward and recognition systems<br>▪ Multiple champions<br>▪ Test-drive changes<br>▪ Management development and executive perspective |

ACTION TOOL 8

## Name That Change!

**Directions:** After you have recorded the type of change you are making, check one of the three boxes on the left and explain why you believe it is that particular type of change. Finally, brainstorm some strategies that would support implementation of this type of change.

**Name Your Change:** _____

**What type of change are you launching?**

**What makes you believe it is that type of change?**

☐ Developmental

_____

☐ Opportunistic

_____

☐ Transformational

_____

**What management techniques and strategies will support successful implementation of this type of change?**

_____

_____

_____

# THE BOTTOM LINE

Organizational changes come in different shapes and sizes. We talk about three types of change in this chapter—developmental change, opportunistic change, and transformational change. The kind of change you are launching has many implications for successful implementation. What (or who) is the source for the change? How does the time frame impact your decisions? Who should lead the change? How should it be managed? Where will resistance originate? What strategies might be appropriate? How strong is the reluctance to commit to this change likely to be? Is it doable within your organizational culture? Is there a better choice?

The practical strategies we suggest for each type of change should give you a good launchpad from which to begin to craft a unique approach to successful implementation. Expect disruptions. Setbacks will occur. Energy will fade. Operational issues will take precedence. If you are convinced that this is the right change, don't let anything dissuade you. How you handle the impending adversity will ultimately determine the success or failure of the initiative.

# Respect the Power of Organizational Culture

*Meaningful change is fad-resistant, and fade-resistant.*
—RICHARD J. DUNSING[1]

In our thirty years of working with organizations to implement change, we have seldom seen the work culture lose a battle! Here's what happens: Most strategic initiatives are mandated (employees are rarely asked to approve them). Most organizations employ well-meaning, compliant people who will try to follow directions, provided they have the know-how. The problem comes when a change diverges too far from the way things are usually done in the organization. Because people have adopted their current values and behaviors over time (doing what they see succeed around them), being asked to do something very different may capture their minds but not their hearts or souls. As a result, they will attempt to comply, but they will not apply their full enthusiasm. Six months after implementation, supervisors are getting 60 percent effort rather than the 100 percent effort needed to achieve the change objective. This is how the battle is lost—halfhearted, reluctant compliance. Either the change falls into a black hole or the organization ends up with a half-effort.

# UNDERSTANDING WORK CULTURE

Everyone has a unique view of what the phrase "work culture" means. This makes culture awkward to properly define, let alone discuss with pragmatic executives. And yet executives have no trouble using the term, and most senior managers respect its power when it comes to helping or hindering change initiatives.

In our consulting work and executive education sessions, we often ask business teams to identify five adjectives that characterize their current work culture. As a follow-up, we ask them to identify five adjectives that characterize the work culture that would best support their business strategy. Without exception, businesspeople can complete these tasks in about three minutes. Even though culture is an ill-defined, mushy subject, most pragmatic thinkers have no trouble describing their organization's present culture or its ideal culture.

What is a work culture? How do organizational cultures differ? Culture has been around since the beginning of organizations, and the attempts to explain and understand this concept have been plentiful over the years. While the topic has experienced a recent rise in interest, work culture is unlike most other business concepts in that it has no single, widely accepted definition. Explanations range from very broad to highly specific. Perhaps that is why authors and consultants always feel a need to develop their own definition.

In the broad sense, work culture encompasses everything from how employees dress to how they make the company's products or services to how they treat each other to how quickly they respond to a customer request. Some samples: Deal and Kennedy define an organization's culture as "the way we do things around here."[2] E. H. Schein describes work culture as "the pattern of basic assumptions that a given group has invented, discovered, or developed in learning to cope with its problems of external adaptation and internal integration."[3] Peters and Waterman describe it as "a dominant and coherent set of shared values conveyed by such symbolic means as stories, myths, legends, slogans, anecdotes, and fairy tales."[4]

Our own thoughts aren't new or earth-shattering, but they represent our experiences with organizations. Here is the definition of work culture that we have gravitated toward:

*Work culture is the basic, common pattern of shared beliefs, values, assumptions, expectations, behaviors, and habits acquired over time by members of the organization. Work culture comprises beliefs (based on values), assumptions (leading to expectations), and behaviors (leading to habits).*

- **Beliefs** are a consistent, organizationally endorsed set of convictions and opinions, based on values and expectations. Generally, beliefs are messages about what people think they should do (intentions). Values represent strong core beliefs.

- **Assumptions** are the unconscious rationale people use to apply beliefs and justify behaviors. Assumptions lead to expectations.

- **Behaviors** are patterns of observable action that constitute the way people operate on a day-to-day basis—how employees conduct themselves. Successful behaviors tend to be repeated—applied to the next similar circumstance. The repeated behaviors become a pattern. If reinforced and continued, the patterns become habits.

You can witness the nature of these shared beliefs, values, assumptions, expectations, behaviors, and habits while touring the facilities of an organization and speaking briefly with some of the people there. Simply notice things like these:

- Attire

- Conversations

- Housekeeping

- Language

- Offices

- Expectations about what works or does not work

- Procedures

- Rituals and traditions

- Signs

- Work pace

Informal descriptions of work culture amount to "how we do things here." If your best friend was hired into your organization, you might go over the unwritten ground rules leading to acceptance in the organization.

> *Little things don't mean a lot—they mean everything.*
> —HARVEY MACKAY[5]

Employees often refer to cultural behavior as the norms of the organization. The term *norm* is the short version for "normal behavior," which is generally described as organizationally acceptable actions. Unwritten ground rules might include provisions like these:

- Always get approval before acting. (Or: Take initiative, then ask for forgiveness.)

- Stay in your area until the boss leaves at 5:15.

- Do not arrive late for meetings.

- Do it right the first time—every time.

- Be aggressive but respectful.

- Don't adopt a change on the first announcement.

- Always decide based on the best interest of the customer.

- Finding ways to save money will get you noticed.

Every organization's pattern is different and it has generally taken years for that pattern to become an accepted, normalized habit demonstrated by the majority of the workforce.

## THE POWER OF WORK CULTURE

Ah, the strength of the collective will of the organizational workforce. The role that work culture plays in implementing change is that of *transfer agent*. When moving from the planning stage (conceiving direction and deciding what needs changing) to the action stage (ensuring the desired behavior) the work culture will both support and transfer the change or act as a block. The work culture will present a green light (go), a yellow light (caution, slow down), or a red light (not now). It will govern and regulate the speed of implementation.

Some changes that organizations want to make are second nature and get automatic green lights. For example:

- Asking employees at Hewlett-Packard to adopt a new piece of innovative hardware

- Asking employees at Microsoft to adopt a new, proven software system

- Asking McDonald's restaurant employees to add a menu item

Changes that align nicely with the organizational culture are readily accepted. Asking for compliance with congruent changes is like asking a duck to swim; it is what comes naturally.

Conversely, some changes that organizations want to make are so counter to the culture that they get an automatic red light. When the communications industry was deregulated, AT&T broke up its business into seven separate companies (the "Baby Bells"). These new entities had to switch from a product service strategy (a monopoly regulated by the government) to a marketing strategy (having to sell products and services in a competitive environment). Even though this new business strategy became an imperative overnight, the culture did not adapt to the change until years later. None of the new entities had built the structure or capability to market and sell products and services. Construction, building switching systems, home repairs, and the like—no problem, that is what they already did, so that came naturally. Effectively "sell"—that will take some time.

> *I came to see, in my time at IBM, that culture isn't just one aspect of the game—it is the game.*
> —LOUIS V. GERSTNER JR.[6]

# CHANGING AT THE SPEED OF CULTURAL FIT

As we suggested earlier, the work culture is the chief regulator of speed. The closer the change is to the existing organizational culture, the quicker the change can be implemented. Since this is a fundamental truth in our study of implementation, it is incumbent on leaders of change to assess the consistency of the work culture with the change they are sponsoring. In general, the greater the disparity between the change requirements and the general characteristics of the work culture, the longer successful implementation will take and the more participation will be needed.

Table 8 provides an illustration of this consistency of work culture with business strategy.

TABLE 8
# Cultural Characteristics That Support Competitive Advantage

| Characteristics of a Supportive Work Culture | |
|---|---|
| **Customer Service** | **Product Attributes** |
| ■ Loyalty | ■ Invention |
| ■ Teamwork | ■ Freedom |
| ■ Good relationships | ■ Individual |
| ■ Understanding | ■ Diversity |
| ■ Consensus | ■ Accomplishment |
| **Cost Orientation** | **Market Dominance** |
| ■ Control | ■ Growth |
| ■ Reliability | ■ Aggressiveness |
| ■ Predictability | ■ Strength |
| ■ Accuracy | ■ Knowledge |
| ■ Improvement | ■ Quickness |

**Note:** We were first introduced to the technique of using employees' adjectives to describe the organizational culture related to competitive advantage by Bill Paul, an internal consultant for Exxon, who presented his ideas at an O.D. Network meeting.

Looking at the table, you may notice that the niche strategy is not represented in this model. We pondered this for a long time but concluded that niche firms represent a truly diverse group. Each firm has fervently pursued a unique market segment, creating its own unique work culture that supports its strategy. We see no common set of cultural characteristics that could be uniformly applied across all successful niche firms, but if we had to choose, we would suggest that the list has to include pride, informality, and product or service quality.

The same principles illustrated in Table 8 apply to an organization change and the need for a supportive work culture. Use Action Tool 9 to gauge to what extent you are "swimming upstream" with your change. To the extent that the adjectives on your two lists are compatible, there may be consistency and a quicker implementation schedule.

## OPTIONS WHEN THE CULTURE AND THE CHANGE ARE MISMATCHED

If your work culture is inconsistent with, nonsupportive of, or counter to the change you want to implement, the sponsor has only a handful of choices available:

- **Change the change.** Some changes can be modified to be less radical and therefore more consistent with the culture. For example, AT&T and the seven Baby Bells might have decided to acquire a leading marketing business or simply outsource marketing rather than scramble to build their own selling capability.

- **Recalibrate your speed of implementation.** The sponsor can develop more realistic time frames to achieve successful implementation. Sometimes a change can be broken into more nearly bite-sized pieces and phased in over time. The judgment to slow down captures the true meaning of changing at the speed of culture fit. AT&T and the Baby Bells might have adjusted their sights to building capability over a six- to ten-year time frame.

ACTION TOOL 9

| **Assessing Work Culture Consistency** | |
|---|---|
| Five adjectives that characterize the current work culture in your company | Five adjectives that characterize the work culture that will best support the implementation of your change |
| _____ | _____ |
| _____ | _____ |
| _____ | _____ |
| _____ | _____ |
| _____ | _____ |

- **Change the work culture.** Reshaping a work culture to fit the change is usually a significant and difficult undertaking. In the case of something as sweeping as an industry deregulation, however, this may be the right approach to take because it's the one most likely to last.

- **Prepare for failure.** Culture inconsistency is not a situation to be quickly managed or manipulated. It is a condition or fact of life. In the short run, implementing a change on time, on budget, and on target when the change runs counter to the culture is virtually impossible.

Two of these options, *recalibrate your speed of implementation* and *change the work culture,* deserve a closer look.

## Recalibrate Your Speed of Implementation

Speed kills! Speed increases the risks. Crashes happen. Everyone knows that. We debated for a long time whether or not to address this topic at all, but since the number one question that our clients ask these days is: "We can't wait that long—how can we do it faster?" we want to provide some general guidance.

> *The time to repair the roof is when the sun is shining.*
> —JOHN F. KENNEDY[7]

In one way, all the chapters in this book have been designed to help you make changes better and with "prudent speed." As we pointed out in Chapter 6, changes vary from process improvements to TQM changes to mergers and acquisitions to strategy shifts to business contractions to cultural changes. Some changes are developmental. Some changes are opportunistic. Some are transformational. Developmental changes are gradual and go on indefinitely. Opportunistic changes have a shorter existence. Transformational changes will take many years to implement successfully. That's just the way it is.

When cultural or individual resistance is what is blocking the change, you may eventually end up forcing compliance, one way or another. But remember, when you are trying to build capability (to gain speed), you must allow some natural processes to run their course. Forcing acceptance through ultimatums and dismissals lowers morale and brings new expenses and learning curves that also take time. Rework drains time and resources. So this is a serious disclaimer: "Speed at your own risk!" Nonetheless, we offer the following suggestions for making changes more quickly.

## When to Go Fast

We noted at the beginning of this chapter that many strategic changes are decided and mandated from the top down. Forcing strategic initiatives is one of the most common reasons such changes often fail. While organizations are not necessarily democracies, behavioral science rules do tend to apply. Employees tend to get committed to initiatives that they help to create!

Mandated changes run the risk of buying bodies but not souls—overtly compliant behavior and covert resistance. They don't inspire employee self-motivation. So why run the risk of such a high failure rate? The answer is, of course, impatience. Participation, involvement, allowance for cultural fit, and mustering resources all take time and a tolerance for complexity and ambiguity. Most senior managers who identify strategic change attach a sense of urgency to gaining the benefits that will result from the change. They allow little time for reflection or insights and have little tolerance for the impact of culture on implementation success.

Despite the dangers of moving too fast, quickening the pace of implementation may be appropriate in conditions like these:

- **Opportunities.** Strategic windows open. Strategic windows close. Such is organizational life. When a window is open and congruent opportunities present themselves, sometimes the best strategy is to seize the day and fix things later as best you can.

- **Cultural fit.** Sometimes a strategic change is flowing with the cultural current. When a change is consistent with the organizational culture, it can be adopted easily and quickly. In this instance, employees are just doing what they already know how to do.

- **Saving the business.** If immediate organizational survival is at stake, the commitment needed for success may be a secondary concern. When mere survival is precarious, if you don't act, there may be no tomorrow.

## When to Go Slowly

Again, in many situations it is imperative to change more cautiously and prudently. Here are some clear examples:

- **Commitment.** When the successful implementation of the change (the intended result) depends on the involvement and commitment of the employees, you must slow down and gain the needed backing. The employees whose support you need must be involved and committed, and they must (correctly) feel that you understand them. In this instance, the sense of ownership is critical.

- **Transformations.** Transformational changes are, by nature, long-term journeys, not short-run fixes. Transformational changes tend to alter the deep structures of the organization, and therefore the learning curve is usually long and must be allowed to unfold.[8]

- **Cultural misfit.** When a strategic change is swimming upstream (it runs counter to the culture), successful implementation is almost never quick and is rarely effective, even if it is mandated.

- **Risk management.** When the pace of the change is too fast to build the capabilities that can sustain a faster pace in the future, it is best to slow down. Risks to employees and resources can result in turnover of key people, equipment and system breakdowns, poor customer service, and rework, all of which are expensive. Anticipate the consequences!

> *Make haste slowly.*
> —AUGUSTUS CAESAR[9]

## Suggestions for Quicker Change

The strategies listed here should help organizations change more quickly while still achieving effective implementation.

- Strongly and clearly articulate the compelling change story.

- Choose the very best project manager and the optimum team of specialists.

- Design, articulate, and communicate a detailed plan for implementation (including the budget and realistic time horizons).

- Acquire all the resources needed for success.

- Monitor the change and follow up continuously.

- Carefully track and liberally publicize progress.

- Praise purposefully, but generously.

## A Final Note on Speed

The disappointing aspect of this issue of speedier changes is the increasingly common belief among organizations that gaining 60 percent of the results of a quick change is the most anyone can expect and is therefore OK. Since effective sponsorship skills and successful implementation practices are not studied and readily known, valued, or developed, getting "a little bit better, quickly" is often seen as acceptable. While quick change seems to be an objective for many, we believe successful, enduring change is a far more productive alternative.

> *I took a course in speed reading and was able to read* War and Peace *in twenty minutes. It's about Russia.*
> —WOODY ALLEN[10]

## Change the Work Culture

If sponsors choose the option of changing the work culture to support the change, they have assumed a significant challenge that will affect every aspect of organizational life. Some examples of points of attack to reshape the work culture:

- **Leadership behavior.** All the leaders and managers involved with reshaping culture must believe in the change and be willing to adjust their behavior to support the change. This modeling requirement includes the enthusiasm to give 100 percent support to the change.

- **Hiring and promotion.** Selection practices must be adjusted to find, hire, and promote people with the traits and characteristics that are identified with the supportive cultural characteristics.

- **Training and development.** Where the new work culture calls for know-how that currently does not exist, training must be provided. Employees cannot change if they do not possess the capability.

- **Customer feedback.** Most people know who pays the company's bills—the customers. Regardless of the competitive advantage being sought, customer buying behavior will be the deciding factor. Acquiring feedback and communicating customer reactions to employees can begin to help shape a new culture.

> *Things do not change; we do.*
> —HENRY DAVID THOREAU[11]

- **Performance measurement.** It is said that people pay attention to what gets measured. Facts and figures expressed by performance metrics and produced on a regular basis can engender new values. Additionally, connecting individual performance expectations to a reward system that supports new behaviors is essential to reshaping the culture.

As you can see, changing the culture to be more consistent with the change requires significant leadership attention and resources.

# THE BOTTOM LINE

It is natural for culture to follow business strategy over time, but it does so at its own speed. Two key variables to the natural reshaping of work culture are age and size. Older and larger organizations tend to be slower in adapting the supportive culture than newer, smaller organizations. Regardless of size and age, however, new practices take time to become shared values.

In a conversation one of us had with Peter Vaill, Peter said that when NASA asked him how long it would take to get back to a zero-defect work culture, he asked, "How long did it take to create zero defect the first time?" NASA answered: "Seven years." Peter said it would take about seven years to get back to zero defect. NASA said: "That's unacceptable. It has to be done in less than two years." Peter said: "I know, but it will still take you seven years if you do the right things and you work very hard at it." In another arena, how long did it take Jack Welch to change the culture at GE? Five years? Seven years? Ten Years? In the short run, mandating work culture values just does not work well. Remember that culture is a condition, not an issue to be easily manipulated.

You can pay now or pay later. If the change and the culture are a mismatch, you will need huge amounts of time, resources, and involvement to succeed. An autocratic change will make implementation a nightmare. On the other hand, a participative change will take a long time up front to gain commitment, but the implementation will go more smoothly.

# Build the Personal
# Case for Change

*Change is exhilarating when done by us,*
*and exasperating when done to us.*
—ROSABETH MOSS KANTER[1]

Exhilarating or exasperating. Isn't that the truth! If it's *my* change, it's a great idea. If it's your change—it's *your* change. . . .

The second potential roadblock to implementation, individual resistance to change, is a common and natural reality of organizational life. Just as you constructed a business case for change to begin to get buy-in, you should now use the materials in this chapter to build a personal case for change. Anticipate people's personal causes for resistance to your change and choose strategies to defuse individual concerns.

You can't manage change the same way you manage stability! The stakes aren't the same. People are anxious about change for myriad reasons. For many employees, change means giving something up. The greater the perceived loss, the more apt these employees are to whine, kick, and scream, drag their feet, dig in their heels, stick a pipe in the spokes, procrastinate, and comply but not commit.

Any organizational change will be viewed by some employees as objectionable. The trick is to make changes and decisions that irritate your worst performers and please your best performers. When the change is successfully implemented (on time, on target, on budget), you want to have retained your good people. Let this thought permeate your actions.

Surprise! The change is not the only thing you must manage. You must help people increase their capacity to handle their day-to-day activities while simultaneously implementing the change. Today's realities suggest that the implementation of any change is being dumped in the laps of people whose plates are already overflowing—especially if your organization has recently experienced a workforce reduction. Whatever you called it—downsizing, rightsizing, reengineering, tightening the belt—many of the survivors see the name as a euphemism for working harder for the same pay.

## (TONGUE IN CHEEK) NAME THAT LOON!

Proposed changes can elicit powerful feelings and reactions that run the gamut from joy to sorrow, excitement to exasperation, frustration to elation, fear to confusion.

> *All mankind is divided into three classes: those who are immovable; those who are movable; and those who move.*
> —BENJAMIN FRANKLIN[2]

Ben Franklin had it right. One simple way to begin to understand individual resistance to change is to notice the initial reactions to an organizational change. If you don't mind our using some stereotypes, most employees can be sorted into three broad groups based on their reactions.[3]

### The Change Fanatics (Those Who Move)

These employees are on board with any change coming down the pike. They don't even need to know what the change is. They like it. They can't comprehend why the organization is not changing faster!

> *A fanatic is someone who can't change his mind and won't change the subject.*
> —SIR WINSTON CHURCHILL[4]

Managers who want to implement a change tend to view employees who pass the zest test as intelligent, savvy, progressive minds. The other employees might perceive the fanatics very differently, with a jaundiced eye, perhaps seeing them as naive, unthinking management patsies.

Just point the fanatics in the right direction and step aside. Of course, you need to be observant and guarded because they see all changes as desirable (even the wrong ones).

## The Staunch Resisters (Those Who Are Immovable)

Staunch resisters are the stubborn, hard-core, die-hard, uncompromising warriors, the sort of whom legends are born. They are the foxhole fraternity, the "hunker down in the bunker" crowd. Wise and wily veterans of past change attempts, they have the battle scars to prove it. These employees love to rally their troops around battle cries of "Heads up; here it comes again!" Additional admonitions might include "There's no salary increase for a purple heart," "Hit the dirt until the mortars stop flying!" or—their ultimate motto—"Chill out! Drag your feet! This too shall pass!" Staunch resisters have seen many changes up close and personal. Changes come and changes go in this organization. They are too cynical to bite on the newest flavor of the month.

Pay attention. Don't contribute to an unfortunate change reaction. These old veterans of past ploys and fuzzy visions are, as we speak, back at the shop, plotting and cloning their young associates to poison the undecided employees. The good news is that these sinister snipers are occasionally correct. Sometimes the change is inappropriate or has no staying power. The bad news is that they are usually wrong. Their critics might say, "Even a blind squirrel finds an acorn every once in a while." Staunch resisters love to intimidate and goad others not to get involved. They may suggest that this new change is a do-it-yourself guillotine kit, for example. Don't give in to the staunch resisters! Show them that this time and this change are different. After delivering a clear message about the change, showing respect for their views, and allowing a fair amount of time for denial, venting, and getting on board with the new direction, you may need to write off the most incorrigible of the staunch resisters.

## The Mystified Masses (Those Who Are Movable)

Most employees are standing on the sidelines, at times amused, at times confused by both the fanatics and the resisters. These are the employees you want to reach. These stupefied spectators are the key! The mystified masses are caught in the middle, uncertain of what to think, uncommitted at the moment, dazed and amazed by both the fanatics and the resisters. They are still gathering information. They are waiting to see what develops before choosing sides. They don't know enough to have taken a solid position yet. Early on, when push comes to shove, they stall a little because they don't want to get involved in this squabble between management, the fanatics, and the staunch resisters.

Offer your best support to the mystified masses. Keep them informed. Tell them the change story over and over. These employees are the key to success!

# KEY IMPLEMENTATION STRATEGIES

Successfully reducing individual resistance to change requires you to change minds—yours and theirs. It's show time! Everyone is watching. Some minds are open, some are closed, some are temporarily under construction. What should you do?

> *Things will get better, despite our efforts to improve them.*
> —WILL ROGERS[5]

Before we begin to unravel the different reasons for resistance, we want to suggest some general implementation strategies (how-to tricks) that you could consider and employ, if and when appropriate. Table 9 presents some specific actions to take before and during the launch of your change. These actions will go a long way toward reducing the impediments lurking in the hallways.

People can probably find any number of reasons to resist change—perhaps more reasons to resist than to comply. However, we believe that most individual resistance to change is caused by one or more of the following six sources: perceived threats, fears, conflicts, distrust, different perceptions, and habits. These reasons for resistance are important, because you can't find a solution (a strategy to reduce individual resistance) until you have clearly identified the problem (why is this person resisting?).

## Perceived Threats

Many employees are reluctant to accept organizational changes because they view the change as a potential threat—a game with a win-lose sum to it. These possible dangers, based on potential perceived losses that may occur with the change, are listed in the left-hand column of Table 10, while the right-hand column lists responses.

TABLE 9
# Key Implementation Strategies[6]

| Prelaunch Strategies | Launch Strategies |
|---|---|
| ■ Anticipate the barriers to implementation. | ■ Acknowledge resistance and resisters. |
| ■ Be a change agent. | ■ Address "I" and "me" issues immediately. |
| ■ Begin to build momentum | ■ Announce the change early to allow time. |
| ■ Challenge people—raise the expectations! | ■ Anchor the change in the organizational culture. |
| ■ Choose the right changes | ■ Clearly explain the case for change again. |
| ■ Form an influential coalition. | ■ Define success of the project. |
| ■ Get resistance out in the open. | ■ Discourage apathy. |
| ■ Involve the opinion leaders. | ■ Don't try to do everything yourself. |
| ■ Look for potential resistance. | ■ Design a supportive environment. |
| ■ Make only the needed changes. | ■ Encourage ownership. |
| ■ Plan ways to reduce impending job stress. | ■ Emphasize the risks of not changing. |
| ■ Remove potential obstacles to the vision. | ■ Encourage the expression of opposition. |
| ■ Sell (but don't oversell) the change. | ■ Engineer some quick wins. |
| ■ Share the case for change. | ■ Establish a mechanism for expressing resistance. |
| | ■ Establish clear priorities. |
| | ■ Illustrate the new opportunities for employees. |
| | ■ Invite participation in implementation. |
| | ■ Model consistent behaviors. |
| | ■ Nail down each person's responsibilities. |
| | ■ Set up a suggestion box for the change. |
| | ■ Stay positive. |
| | ■ Take all objections seriously. |
| | ■ Take ownership. |

**Note:** These strategies are a collage from our own experiences and ideas presented in Price Pritchett and Ron Pound, *Business as Unusual: The Handbook for Managing & Supervising Organizational Change* (EPS Solutions, 1994); and Colin Bainbridge, *Designing for Change: A Practical Guide to Business Transformation* (New York: Wiley, 1996).

TABLE 10
## Resistance Caused by Perceived Threats

| Perceived Threats—Feelings of Loss | Potentially Helpful Strategies |
|---|---|
| ■ Loss of affiliation<br>■ Loss of confidence<br>■ Loss of power or status<br>■ Loss of resources<br>■ Loss of security or comfort | ■ Accept management responsibility for past failures.<br>■ Acknowledge the loss with a celebration to gain closure.<br>■ Actively listen to employees; their perceptions may not match management's.<br>■ Present potential scenarios showing the benefits of the change.<br>■ Present positive personal development plans.<br>■ Stress improved job prospects. |

## Fears

It is natural for employees to feel trepidation about swimming in unfamiliar waters. The status quo brings comfort. The unknown brings anxiety. Employees question whether they can handle the new skills and demands. They also wonder about the increased expectations that often accompany changes. Table 11 balances these fears with suggested helpful strategies.

## Conflicts

Potential disagreements are another possible reason for individual resistance to change. Conflicting roles, goals, and expectations may surface. Use the strategies in Table 12 to counter them.

## Distrust

The fourth common area of individual resistance stems from lack of faith in the change, the sponsor, management, or the employee's immediate supervisor. Table 13 presents a summary of distrust items with corresponding ways to build trust.

## Different Perceptions

The fifth widespread possibility for individual resistance is the tendency for everyone to see the need for change, the appropriateness of this change, and the meaningfulness of this change differently. Table 14 presents the different percep-

> *Silence is one of the hardest arguments to refute.*
> —JOSH BILLINGS[7]

tions people may have in the midst of organizational change, along with strategies to help align those perceptions with organizational goals.

TABLE 11
## Resistance Caused by Fears

| Fears | Potentially Helpful Strategies |
|---|---|
| ▪ Fear of the unknown (ambiguity)<br>▪ Fear of success (more work, higher expectations)<br>▪ Fear of failure (feelings of inadequacy) | ▪ Admit your own fears and describe what convinced you to ignore them.<br>▪ Address individual fears openly and honestly.<br>▪ Be positive and enthusiastic.<br>▪ Establish support groups.<br>▪ Explain what the change means for individuals.<br>▪ Express confidence in their ability to succeed.<br>▪ Explain why personal advantages outweigh disadvantages.<br>▪ Encourage and support any needed training.<br>▪ Involve people in positive, quick-turnaround action.<br>▪ Persuade people that change will mean opportunities.<br>▪ Try to reinforce the idea that fear of the status quo should be greater than fear of change. |

TABLE 12
## Resistance Caused by Conflicts

| Conflicts | Potentially Helpful Strategies |
|---|---|
| ■ Conflicting roles | ■ Allow for constructive exceptions. |
| ■ Conflicting goals | ■ Be open to modifications. |
| ■ Control issues | ■ Build rapport outside work. |
| ■ Functional perspectives | ■ Create discontent with the conflict in the present situation. |
| ■ Group loyalties | |
| ■ Power plays | ■ Clearly communicate the need for change. |
| ■ Revenge | ■ Emphasize the areas of agreement. |
| ■ Turf battles | ■ Honor the conflicting parties and negotiate resolutions. |
| ■ Saving face | |
| | ■ Involve all functional areas in the planning. |
| | ■ Practice full disclosure to build trust. |
| | ■ Use role-playing exercises. |

## Habits

A final reason for individual resistance to change is habits. The more you repeat the steps in a job, the easier the job becomes. Learning a new set of steps makes the job harder. Unless they're offered more pay, most people would prefer to do easier work.

> *It is impossible to persuade a man who doesn't disagree, but smiles.*
> —MURIEL SPARK[8]

Habits can be very powerful forces. For example, both of us, who grew up when cars had carburetors that needed to be primed, still pump the gas pedal before turning over the engine—even though the instruction manuals for fuel-injected cars clearly say not to do that!

Action Tool 10 gives you the opportunity to anticipate and plan for the individual resistance your change is likely to encounter.

TABLE 13
# Resistance Caused by Distrust

| Distrust | Potentially Helpful Strategies |
|---|---|
| <ul><li>Of the change</li><li>Of the change agent</li><li>Of management</li><li>Of the immediate superior</li></ul> | <ul><li>Admit past mistakes and explain how they will be avoided this time.</li><li>Answer every question to the inquirer's satisfaction.</li><li>Be open, honest, and thorough.</li><li>Carefully explain the reasons for the change.</li><li>Demonstrate (using examples) why the old ways won't work anymore.</li><li>Emphasize past successes.</li><li>Hold meetings to communicate the details of the change agenda.</li><li>Invite and seek involvement.</li></ul> |

TABLE 14
# Resistance Caused by Different Perceptions

| Different Perceptions | Potentially Helpful Strategies |
|---|---|
| <ul><li>Different assessments of the need for change</li><li>Different views of the appropriateness of this change</li><li>Different judgments of the meaningfulness of this change (is it just the flavor of the month?)</li></ul> | <ul><li>Clarify any perceived role or goal conflicts.</li><li>Explain the plan with greater clarity and detail.</li><li>Explain what would happen if the company didn't change.</li><li>Help employees weigh pros and cons of the alternatives.</li><li>Involve everyone in implementation teams.</li><li>Show why the new change is sustainable and not a fad.</li><li>Use a bottom-up process for adapting systems and procedures to facilitate the change.</li></ul> |

# MINIMIZE THE PLUNGE OF ALLEGIANCE AFTER LAYOFFS

Before we finish with this topic, we should give you a look at another tough leadership issue closely connected to the challenges presented by the six reasons for individual resistance.

Unfortunately, the global economy has been emerging in fits and starts, rather than rising in a smooth tide that brings prosperity everywhere. The dysfunctions of the process have resulted in some massive workforce reductions. Successfully launching, sustaining, and completing changes that require large personnel cuts may be the hardest change leadership job of all.

## Drastic Changes Are Afoot!

The organizational landscape is continuing to be redrawn as we write this. Product obsolescence, market shifts, new technologies, and intensifying competition are causing rightsizings, mergers, acquisitions, takeovers, strategic alliances, bankruptcies, and reorganizations. When one of these euphemistic tragedies strikes close to home, with you or your friends as the victims, the reactions are hardly passé. Nervous queries flutter like confetti through the corridors. Many of the victims are devastated. Many survivors are shaken. The human reactions to a massive layoff often range from alarm to pity, from anger to sorrow, from fear to resignation, from resentment to gloom.

> *Success has many fathers, failures have none.*
> —PHILIP CALDWELL[9]

In times of pain, shock, and uncertainty, employees need information, support, and answers. Some typical laments we hear: Why? What in the world happened? Is this just the tip of the iceberg? Is there another bombshell coming? Employees want to know why these decisions were made, how they were made, and how future decisions will be made. What happens next? How will the remaining employees function after the fall? Did the bosses cut fat or muscle? Does every survivor now get three jobs for one salary as a reward for still being employed?

Remember the adage "Fool me once, shame on you; fool me twice, shame on me"? This phrase may be on the lips of some of your best people. They are watching and waiting. Remember, your best employees have options! Drastic

ACTION TOOL 10

## Planning for Individual Resistance

**Directions:** What individual resistance will your change encounter? Rank the anticipated causes of individual resistance to your change.

**Rating Key**
**1** = the highest anticipated reason; **5** = the lowest anticipated reason

| **Reason for Resistance** | **Rank** |
|---|---|
| Conflicts | _____ |
| Different perceptions | _____ |
| Distrust | _____ |
| Fears | _____ |
| Perceived threats | _____ |
| Habits | _____ |

How can you discover the real order? Why not survey some of the employees? Which ones?

_____

_____

List two strategies that you will implement for each cause.

**Reason for Resistance**          **Strategies to Lower Resistance**

Conflicts                          1. _____

                                   2. _____

Different perceptions              1. _____

                                   2. _____

Distrust                           1. _____

                                   2. _____

ACTION TOOL 10 (cont'd)

| Reason for Resistance | Strategies to Lower Resistance |
|---|---|
| Fears | 1. _____ |
| | 2. _____ |
| Perceived threats | 1. _____ |
| | 2. _____ |
| Habits | 1. _____ |
| | 2. _____ |

change requires enormous and thoughtful preparation if you want to retain your best people and regain the loyalty of the survivors. Cultural and individual resistance are usually the main obstacles to a return to some degree of normalcy.

> *Man is the only animal that blushes. Or needs to.*
> —MARK TWAIN[10]

Whatever the reasons for the downsizing, after a large workforce cut, many of the people who are still employed have doubts, guilt, and feelings of betrayal. The victims of the cuts were their friends, relatives, and colleagues. The rational, realistic employees have a new mantra: There, but for the grace of God, go I.

## Rebuilding the Survivors' Loyalty

There is no doubt that any major cutback will damage employee loyalty and morale.[11] The only questions are, How much? and For how long? The ability of the organization to keep the flood waters at bay, to stabilize and rebuild credibility, will usually depend on the survivors' perception of the answers to some very basic questions:

### Question 1: What in the world happened?
Was this calamity avoidable? Did we lose a huge order? Did demand disappear and sales plummet? Were we grossly inefficient? Were our costs too high?

It is easier for the remaining employees to understand the need for change if high labor costs or major inefficiencies were the cause. But if top management made strategic blunders that resulted in the reductions, morale and loyalty will be more difficult to rebuild.

*Answer*

Don't fudge here. Show authentic concern and empathy. Restate the business case! Be open, honest, informative, straightforward, and clear about the drivers for this change—and don't try to shift the blame.

## Question 2: Was there another way?

Were these cuts the best possible option? Were they necessary? Sometimes organizations have little choice about making the change. Other times, there are several options. Remember the situation—it is hard for survivors to accept layoffs, dismissals, and salary cuts when the management isn't sharing in the pain. Common sense should prevail. Management's credibility is at stake.

*Answer*

Use the business case to explain the sequence of events, the available alternatives, and why this change was the most viable option. Make sure that everyone shares fairly in this burden.

## Question 3: What were the criteria for choosing the survivors?

If you can build a strong case for the drastic action, the next issue becomes who is being dismissed and who is being retained. What was used to determine the winners and losers? Seniority? Performance? Costs? Were the criteria appropriate? Were they applied consistently?

Firing the highest-paid (most successful) employees may save the most money, but it sends the wrong message to the survivors. Work hard, do what is asked, perform well, and you will be rewarded by becoming prime fodder for the chopping block. What kind of incentive is that?

*Answer*

Cuts should be consistent with your historical performance criteria. Perhaps seniority should win the close calls. Remember, whatever criteria you use, anticipate the consequences. At this traumatic moment, your actions are symbolic—they send clear messages. Choosing an inappropriate set of guidelines can fuel an already volatile situation.

### Question 4: What is the organization doing to help the displaced workers?

Most survivors can understand necessary economic actions. But they will watch to see if the company cares. In particular, they will be interested in how much the company is doing, how many resources are being assigned to help the displaced employees cope, recover, and find meaningful employment elsewhere. The savvy survivors are mumbling, "That could have been (perhaps should have been) me!"

*Answer*

Set up all the helpful processes you can envision. Benchmark what other organizations have done to cope with drastic cuts successfully. Bring in counselors to help people with the psychological aspects of rejection and the grief process. Investigate and post current employment opportunities. Assist employees with résumé writing and interviewing techniques. Do the right things!

### Question 5: How well is the change process being communicated?

Don't wimp out and practice mushroom management (keep them in the dark and feed them fertilizer) because you are afraid to own up to the truth or because communicating well is painful and expensive. The survivors are watching to see if you really care about their needs.

*Answer*

Practice full disclosure. Share any important information regarding the change. What do employees know? What do they need to know? What is being clearly explained in written form? How is the grapevine being managed?

### Question 6: Why should the survivors believe that the future will be any different?

Future loyalty depends on three things:

- How truthful the organization is at this critical juncture

- How fair the criteria to determine the survivors were

- How unlikely it is that this event will be repeated in the future

*Answer*

Design and clearly communicate specific strategies that are being implemented to reduce the possibility of this recurring. For example, will the company job out work rather than add staff? Work overtime rather than add staff? Have everyone take a slight reduction rather than let more people go? What's the plan?

The survivors want to know that specific strategies are being put in place to minimize the chance of a repeat performance. Having a plan to minimize the organization's susceptibility to business cycles and shifts in competitive winds shows that the leaders care about the survivors. Even if people weren't asking for it, you should do it anyway because it is the right thing to do. No organization can guarantee what the future will bring. The survivors know that. They just want to believe that management is honestly trying to look ahead.

## Question 7: What is the organization doing to heal the wounds of the survivors?

Friends, perhaps relatives, have been thrown out in the street. Close relationships have been ripped apart. It is now a whole new milieu. Climate shifts are drifting through the corridors. Helping the survivors adjust is the first step to a new beginning.

Unfortunately, some companies are ignorant of the human impact, or too fearful of showing feelings to do any more than say something like, "You're lucky you're still here. Now go out and get the job done." We don't know about you, but that doesn't make us feel all warm and fuzzy. In fact, we don't think we would stick around to be used and abused. If you're on the receiving end, run, don't walk, to the nearest headhunter or job search site—it's time to leave this pup tent to its own demise! If you're contemplating sending such a message, remember that you don't need to lose very many of your really good employees before you will become uncompetitive.

### Answer

Actions, not words, can help reduce the potential distrust. Implement some sensible, caring, respectful healing strategies. Why not settle on the optimum staff level and institute some form of employment security program based on performance? Perhaps you could initiate a probationary period, after which the really good performers are guaranteed a job. Maybe, during normal economic downturns, the core group of employees is guaranteed 75 percent of their base earnings. The upside here is that when demand is up, employees will be more likely to do whatever is needed. Why not begin to establish a contingency fund from which employees could draw

> *To finish first, you must first finish.*
> —RICK MEARS[12]

during periods of slack demand? Why not involve the survivors in designing and implementing strategies to maintain the stability of the workforce? You might be pleasantly surprised at what they invent. Design what is best for your firm and new culture, but be caring and creative.

## Rekindling Loyalty

Keeping the best employees on board and productive during large reductions in the workforce may be the true test of an organization's leadership. Action Tool 11 is designed to help you recall strategies for regaining lost loyalties.

# THE BOTTOM LINE

Resistance to change takes time, energy, and even creativity. Managing resistance takes time, energy, and even more creativity. The real leadership genius is to find more productive ways to channel this energy and creativity, and then make it happen. If you're running into a wall, diagnose the source of the resistance and give the actions we suggest here a try!

No matter what you do, you can be sure that the implementation process won't go entirely smoothly. Somewhere along the line, a few projects will falter. The key to success is what happens then. What are you going to do at that moment? Quickly! A failure message is sweeping down the hallways. Point to the successes. Explain how you will make adjustments to prevent setbacks in the future.

Somewhere along the implementation journey, people will lose focus. What are you going to do at that moment? Quickly! The staunch resisters are stirring and scolding—"We told you it would pass!" Clearly restate the case for change. Revisit the vision. Make the goal the boss.

Somewhere along that same trek

- Operational issues will take short-run priority

- Energy will ebb

Less certain, but still probable

- A few of your good people may leave

- You may get acquired, merged, or caught up in a new alliance

ACTION TOOL 11

## Learning from Layoffs

**Directions:** After you have considered the problem of layoffs and lost loyalties, answer the following questions in the space provided.

1. Have you ever experienced a severe personnel reduction? If you have, what did you learn from the experience that might help you help or protect your direct reports? If you haven't experienced this phenomenon, what was your organization doing that might be transferable to your current situation?

   _____

   _____

   _____

2. See if you can invent three truly unusual, creative strategies to regain lost loyalties.

   _____

   _____

   _____

Here's our advice for coping with any of these possibilities: Be cautious. Don't declare the change a success too soon! As Yogi Berra said, It ain't over till it's over.

In general, the keys to overcoming individual resistance to any kind of change are education (about the need for and results of the change), communication (all along the way, with every involved group), participation (at all levels with all affected groups), and support (by making only needed changes, announcing them in advance, providing any needed training, and giving people a fair amount of time to adjust to the change).

Help people cope, learn, change, and get on board. Show respect. Be fair—and be patient. However, sooner or later, this train is leaving the station for the new promised land. The moment will come when you shout "All aboard," the whistle blows, and the train starts moving. At that moment, anyone who is not on board will be left standing at the station. So be it! Leave them there. Wave good-bye. Wish them luck. The folks on the train have got work to do and a successful implementation to finish.

# 9

# Choose the Right Sponsor for the Change

*Do not put the saddle on the wrong horse.*
—ENGLISH PROVERB

Who is the best person to lead this change? Who has the most credibility related to the change? Who has the appropriate talent? Who has the desire? Who has the time? Who could shepherd the employees down the right path and reach the right destination?

## STAMPING THE BIG R ON SOMEONE'S FOREHEAD!

Whether you call the leader of the change the sponsor, champion, czar, change manager, or program manager, the best way to assure the implementation of a strategic change is to clearly assign the responsibility (the Big R) to *one person*. As one senior manager said in a staff meeting, "When I look around the table, I have to know where my eyes should stop." He used these change leadership rules:

- Every strategic initiative will have *one sponsor* who is responsible for implementation.

- All his sponsors must come from his direct report staff.

- Sponsors do not have to do all the work. It's OK to have a project manager to do the heavy lifting, but the sponsor is the person responsible for on-time, on-budget, on-target progress until the change has been completely implemented and turned over to a process manager for maintenance.

This senior manager allowed no exceptions to these rules, and sponsors reported on their progress once a month. Every year, they established 25 top priority changes that would support the strategic success of their business unit. After the first year they had implemented 30 percent of their strategic initiatives. By the end of their third year the implementation rate was at 75 percent, and it increased to 80 percent by the end of year four. Not only were the sponsors completing a high percentage, but the quality of implementation was so high that they were among industry leaders in business results.

This particular leader understood the significance of the idea that today competes with tomorrow (see Figure 1, on page 9). He knew that the pressure to meet today's business and financial targets puts enormous strain on time and resources. He also knew that if preparations for the future receive little time or attention, there might not be a tomorrow. Balancing this paradox, the conflict of resource allocation between today's results and tomorrow's planning, was critical to him. Day-to-day dialogue was usually centered on operations. But every month (with no exceptions) he and his direct reports had a serious dialogue about implementing strategic change. It took about two years for the team to learn to manage their calendars so that their operational and sponsorship duties were performed well.

One study reported that 75 percent of the mergers and acquisitions the researchers studied were failures.[1] Similarly, in a study of more than two hundred North American companies, when all types of changes were combined, the results showed a 25 percent success rate.[2] In general, the professional literature seems to suggest that somewhere between two-thirds and three-fourths of all change efforts end in some kind of failure. Our own experiences support these findings. We further believe that inadequate leadership (sponsorship) causes perhaps a quarter of those failures.

Trying to determine if these numbers are perfectly accurate misses the point. The estimates are in the right ballpark and the message is clear: leading the implementation of strategic change is critically important to success. This chapter provides insight into that leadership role.

> *Be not afraid of going slowly; be only afraid of standing still.*
> —CHINESE PROVERB

## SO, WHAT IS A SPONSOR'S JOB?

From our point of view, there are three important roles in leading a strategic change initiative—leader, facilitator, and manager—and being able to move from one role to another at the appropriate time requires experience. Let's look at each of these roles.

### Leader

*Leadership* is defined here as the process of influencing others. The folks in the organization are counting on the leader to select the right business strategies and the changes to pursue. The cost of selecting the wrong change to implement is enormous when you think about the resources taken from today's productivity. The organization must select the right change and the right sponsor, who must articulate the business case in the right way: the way that is compelling and truthful and speaks not only to the minds but also to the hearts of the employees. This role also requires being able to understand complexity (during implementation) in such a way that those who are confused can see a perspective that simplifies the situation and eases their anxiety and paralysis. The sponsor should have the capacity to understand and speak about the big picture (at the 50,000-foot level) as well as the meaning the change has to an individual job holder (at sea level). This kind of mental agility and shifting perspective typically comes from some experience with leading change implementations.

### Facilitator

*Facilitator* literally means one who makes things easy. Skills related to providing know-how, reducing individual resistance, and conducting effective meetings become essential for dealing with cultural shaping. What facilitators do is engage change targets (those who will feel the impact of the change) in developing ideas that support effective implementation. Specifically, good facilitators brainstorm solutions, get agreement to action, determine measurements, encourage involvement, and listen intently. The facilitator role, along with the leader role, provides the skills and opportunity for developing true buy-in and commitment. You cannot overestimate the value of collaboration through meetings that are skillfully crafted and conducted.

## Manager

Being the manager primarily involves organizing the project and exhibiting skills related to rerailing action plans that are off schedule, off budget, or off track. This role acknowledges that this particular change has never been done before in this organization. As a result, people face a learning curve. The assumption is that change will not go exactly according to the plan. The trick is to know quickly when people are getting off plan and rerail the process with adjustments.

The ability to rerail quickly requires two elements. First, the organization needs a clear project plan that includes milestone achievements, target dates for completion, and responsibility for action. This plan can be a simple form or a more comprehensive, automated program (many project management software systems are on the market). The second requirement is some kind of monitoring process. Remember the senior management team that opened the chapter, meeting every month . . . face-to-face . . . no exceptions. Persistence is a necessity, not a luxury, in the successful implementation of change. Managers push to meet schedules, solve problems, find resources, call in favors, and invent creative ways to achieve objectives.

So what is the sponsor's job? It is to build and articulate the plan, inspire optimism, involve people, build commitment, and assure the maintenance of the momentum to achieve implementation.

# WHAT ARE THE QUALIFICATIONS FOR A GREAT SPONSOR?

Not everyone is a good candidate to sponsor the implementation of strategic initiatives. Understanding the three roles of leader, facilitator, and manager, and when to practice each role, requires a mature, perceptive person. Our suggestions for the competencies (knowledge, skills, abilities) necessary to perform the three roles are shown in Table 15.

TABLE 15
# Competency Requirements for Sponsors

## Leadership Capabilities

**The Ability to Influence:** A successful sponsor usually has great influence, based on three types of power.

- *Appropriate Positional Power:* Holds an influential position in the organization. The shepherd needs enough rank and status within an organization to command attention and allocate resources. Having the right level of authority is essential to providing the perception of the importance of the change and to being able to make decisions.

- *Abundant Personal Power:* Demonstrates an attractive personality. The shepherd also needs to be someone employees are drawn to, making successful implementation easier.

- *Superior Technical Expertise:* Manifests exceptional subject matter knowledge. Expertise is probably the single most important base of influence in organizations.

**Change Leadership Credibility:** Has a reputation and a history or track record for successfully implementing strategic initiatives in the past. It makes a huge difference in the confidence level when the leader has a reputation for successful implementation.

**Sensitivity Skills:** Actions indicate caring about both the business case and the feelings and needs of others. The sponsor needs maturity to get beyond selfishness and engage the minds and hearts of the employees.

**Communication Skills:** Effectively expresses the vision, plans, and critical decisions. The sponsor should also be articulate and able to provide both technical and human support.

**Cultural Perceptiveness Competencies:** Understands the needs and the power of the work culture to creatively and enthusiastically support change or push changes into the black hole. The sponsor should have the skill to shape the work culture to support the change.

**Behavioral Skills:** Displays the maturity and security to be able to do the right thing at the right time. (Competence, by itself, is not enough.) Enables others through awareness of personal biases, tendencies, and behavior patterns. The sponsor believes in the change and is willing to be the first to adapt to it.

TABLE 15 (cont'd)

## Facilitator Capabilities

**Listening Skills:** Tries to understand others' perspectives, practices total listening concentration, removes distractions, exhibits empathy, responds to feelings, remains objective, asks for clarification, provides closure to issues that represent group consensus.

**Self-Esteem Skills:** Encourages involvement, shows respect, brainstorms possibilities, acts authentically, recognizes accomplishments, expresses confidence, shares thoughts and feelings, practices full disclosure, provides support without removing responsibility, and rewards and inspires others.

**Catalyst Skills:** Inspires actions, maintains a broad perspective, coaches others to take initiative, believes in enabling others to take personal responsibility for getting things done.

## Management Capabilities

**Planning Skills:** Adept at shifting from broad vision to implementation details. Maintains a positive, determined perspective. Creates and clearly articulates a shared vision for the change. Cooperatively establishes the specific goals (targets) and the strategies (the means), along with a project time table with checkpoints.

**Organizing Skills:** Coordinates (groups) people, activities, and resources to successfully accomplish the change. Uses the change objectives as the basis for deciding how to structure the project.

**Monitoring Skills:** Sets benchmarks. Carefully controls progress by checking and correcting the progress being made toward the change goals.

**Change Expertise Skills:** Exhibits knowledge, skills, and proficiencies in specific areas related to leading change. Shows resilience. Handles success, disappointment, rejection, and failure while maintaining effectiveness. Rerails initiatives with creative solutions; maintains control.

Leadership, facilitation, and management skills are the prerequisites—they qualify people to be on the short list of candidates for sponsorship of the strategic initiative.

Selecting the right person to sponsor a strategic change is one of those critical decisions that make or break successful implementation. Finding the right skill, ability, and performance record to match change requirements is almost a science. The final selection of the right shepherd for the specific change is yours! Once the sponsor has been named, the real art begins.

# EFFECTIVE CHANGE MANAGEMENT PRACTICES

There are at least two things you can be fairly certain of in the world of organizations:

- The future will bring a large amount of change.

- Any deliberate attempt at strategic change will inevitably get derailed during the course of implementation.

The reasons for derailment are often multiple (cultural incompatibility, individual resistance, inadequate sponsorship, silo barriers, and resource constraints). But at the core of the roadblocks are habits and the learning curve. Any new change implementation brings with it unfamiliarity. The organization has never done it before. Employees have never done it before. Sponsors should expect derailing of the change to occur from inside and outside the organization. The only questions are what the source of resistance is likely to be and how often the change will get derailed. Therefore, the rerailing skills of the sponsor become critical.

## Sponsor Philosophy

It is fitting at this point to explore the issue of sponsor philosophy. Most of the highly effective executives we know are driven by a philosophy that strongly values high performance. They set the bar high, expecting and often demanding exceptional levels of performance. They incessantly drive organizational performance. This demanding dimension of sponsor style is a double-edged sword. When things are going well it usually evokes unparalleled levels of achievement, satisfaction, and a warranted sense of pride.

When things do not go so well, however, people often feel a burden of guilt for letting down their leader (whom they want to please) and themselves. If the bar is set so high that it is realistically unattainable, this not-measuring-up pattern wears people down and can erode accountability. People begin to avoid controversial issues and affix blame elsewhere because nothing is ever good enough. Applying this pressure for top performance needs context. For day-to-day operations where organizational capability is strong, erring on the side that sets the bar high is a good risk. For significant change efforts, setting a world-class standard immediately will probably run the risk of a negative reaction.

## Surprise Events

Why do things often go poorly during change efforts? We have already cited the learning curve as one reason. There is an important second cause. *Something unexpected will happen!* During the course of the change cycle, especially during the implementation of the change, unpredictable things will always happen.

To unravel this phenomenon of surprise events, take a look at the change cycle and the implications of those events. Our version of the change cycle that leads to resistance and failure is presented in Figure 3. The second change cycle, presented in Figure 4, is the version we believe will lead to greater success. You might notice some of the similarities between the failure cycle and the work of Elisabeth Kübler Ross concerning the "grief cycle."[3] The feelings experienced are similar after something unexpected happens, because loss is experienced in both cases. Also, the work of William Bridges on endings and new beginnings[4] underscores the components in both cycles.

A change effort always begins with a new opportunity or possibility (an idea). As discussed, the stimulation for the new possibility can stem from external drivers, the pursuit of competitive advantage, or the search for internal organizational fitness. Regardless of the source, a new opportunity, idea, or possibility is at the origin of the change cycle. This awareness typically carries with it a feeling of hope and power for those who see the new possibility.

Here's an example to illustrate this cycle. Assume (we're not admitting anything) that we're seriously overweight. Suppose it were to occur to us that we could live a happier life at a more normal, more healthy weight. If that idea holds enough promise, we create or discover a plan (how much and how to) that takes our feelings to a heightened level of enthusiasm. Now we feel

FIGURE 3

# The Path to Failure

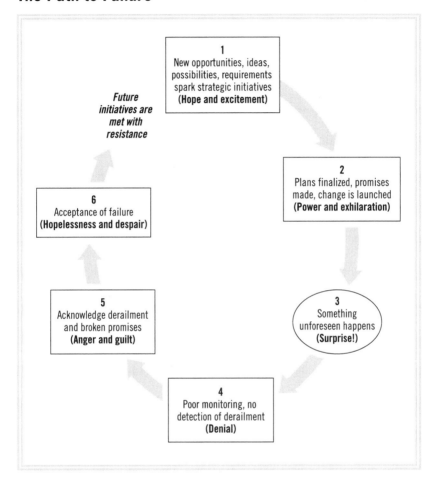

excitement and exhilaration because we believe this can go from the idea stage to reality. For example, we may hear about a diet that fits the bill. We really think we can live with this solution for the long run, so we decide to implement the diet plan.

It is during implementation that something always happens. In this example, say we go to a party or a great social event. The food is marvelous. We have a bad craving. We go off the diet. In business, the unexpected event could be a budget cut, a reduction in force, severe cultural resistance, a lost account, a reorganization, or a competitor announcing a product innovation.

FIGURE 4
# The Path to Success

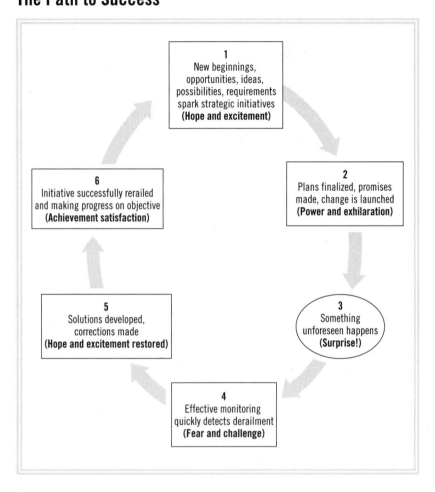

Stuff always happens. It always will. New stuff will cause us to take our eye off the ball (successful implementation).

Once a change has been derailed, typical questions become

- Did we anticipate well?

- How well planned was the change?

- Did we devise and employ strategies to lessen the impact?

- How good is our monitoring and correction system?

If the derailment is not detected quickly, the process will enter a period of muddling through, where the implementation falters. Even if the derailment is detected, there may be a short period of denial. We may not want to acknowledge that we are indeed off plan.

When we finally do recognize and are willing to admit that we are no longer on target, we must face the reality that we have shattered others' expectations and broken some promises. We may well feel frustration, guilt, or anger for not having the foresight, the will, the fortitude, and the persistence to bypass the derailment and get the change rerailed.

The final stage of the failure cycle is settling in on the reality that the new possibility we were so hopeful about may not happen. Failure is a quiet time of loneliness, blame placing, despair, and hopelessness. In the example of the personal diet plan, the sentiment is that we really thought it was that diet plan that could take us to the Promised Land of Normal Weight. For organizations, the pattern is the same. We had a good original idea, but it faded into the black hole of change.

It is this failure cycle that begins with an emotional high and then leads to an emotional low that creates reputations for sponsors. Do they lead change well? Or poorly? You do not have to take people through the fail cycle too many times (two or three will do it) before they say no to Stage 1 (new possibility). Veterans create new resisters. "Don't take me down that change road again. It always leads to the black hole and bad feelings. World without end. Let's not get started."

This cycle of despair and resistance necessitates that sponsors be highly effective rerailers. To earn the reputation of being effective, a sponsor needs to open up a different cycle. As one executive puts it, "I never get upset with my sponsors for being derailed. It is to be expected. In fact I reward the acknowledgment. What makes me angry is being in the slog-along period too long or, worse, trying to hide it." The cycle this change leader utilized had four steps: plan, do, evaluate, and adjust. A good evaluation process discovers any derailment, and its planning adjustments provide a picture of the rerailment needs.

## GUIDANCE TO HELP OTHERS COPE WITH CHANGE

Sponsors can play a large part in enabling employees to cope with change. Here are a half-dozen suggestions that sponsors might find useful.

- **Move prudently into the future.** Relax. Take a deep breath. Take your time. Be patient. The natural tendency is to rush the change to get it out of the way. Haste doesn't seem to work very well with organizational change. You may ultimately go faster if you don't hurry the steps. Transitions stir up a lot of muck and debris. Fears, anxieties, and insecurities need some time to work themselves out, and comfort zones and relationships need time to reestablish themselves.

- **Accentuate the positive.** Stay focused on the opportunities. Change can bring great new possibilities. Seek out the potential advantages. Stay positive. Keep an upbeat, open mind. Negativism is like a contagious disease. When you look for potential benefits, you may be pleasantly surprised.

- **Ask for what you need.** Change brings new challenges. Change requires new skills, new learning. It is natural to not have all the answers. Don't be reluctant to seek advice, support, or assistance.

- **Work out.** Reenergize. When you get bogged down, you need to clear your mind. Why not go for a jog? Take a walk? Go hiking? Pump some iron? Play racquetball, tennis, or golf? Go to a baseball game? If you aren't into exercise, why not visit the museum or sit in the park to clear your head?

- **Keep one eye on today and the other eye on tomorrow.** Don't live in the past. Live in the present with one eye on the future. Try doing something new. No fear. Think of something new you have wanted to try for a while. Do it!

- **Celebrate.** Blood, sweat, and cheers! When you have made some progress, it's time to be good to yourself. Perhaps you should buy that item you have been eyeing for some time. Maybe you should plan a small trip. The best way to do this is to set up the reward ahead of time. You can use it as your incentive to make progress on your change journey.

# THE BOTTOM LINE

This chapter enumerates several qualifications and hurdles to be overcome by the sponsor, then describes the practices necessary to be an effective shepherd of change. We have four final thoughts that may be helpful.

- **Adopt the right values.** Sponsors must believe that the strategic change they are leading is in the best interest of the enterprise, has adequate payback if implemented successfully, and is ethically congruent with their own values. This congruence permits an authentic passion for the change that can be seen in action. This becomes true walking the talk . . . from the inside.

- **Make a good first appearance.** First impressions count. Getting off to a false start hurts. You do not want your first great act of implementation to be a save . . . a rerailment. Accurately assessing what type of change this is can help you avoid starting in the wrong place. Remember, the approaches to developmental, opportunistic, and transformational change are very different.

> *One of the highest—and most beneficial—accolades for a manager is the comment, If he (or she) says so, you can bank on it!*
> —JAMES L. HAYES[5]

- **Build your reputation.** Ultimately, sponsors want to build a strong reputation for implementing important changes on time, on budget, and on target. By achieving those results three or four times in a row, you will have earned the status of supreme sponsor. To reach this level requires practicing some of the important techniques covered in this book: communicate the right things, always listen to feedback (especially constructive criticism), provide training, acquire resources, follow a monitoring discipline that surfaces derailments, and efficiently rerail.

- **Practice the art.** The science of effective sponsorship goes only so far; then the art of leadership must take over. When should you use the power of your office? When is it appropriate to defuse a situation with humor? When is the best time to put a new perspective on the change? When should you listen and nurture? When can you express disappointment without incurring a penalty? In the end, if you are fortunate enough to be charismatic, your natural appeal and charm can go a long way toward successful implementation.

# 10

# Tear Down
# Those Silos!

*Make three correct guesses consecutively and you
will establish a reputation as an expert.*
—LAURENCE J. PETER[1]

Another potential barrier to the successful implementation of any change is
the division of the organization into silos. The grouping of the same or similar tasks (creating pockets of specialized knowledge) provides distinct opportunities for the disruption of the seamless implementation of new strategic
initiatives.

## A PARABLE

A short time ago, in a galaxy not far away . . . motley bands of organizational
dwellers began to congregate and huddle in groups of like kinds. These cov-
eys willingly but unknowingly planted and cultivated the seeds of balkanized
fiefdoms as they successfully profited from the promised fruits of specialized
labor. Haughty high priests of minute practices became highly regarded and
highly rewarded. And the crop was good and the clusters were baptized,

grew, and bred, and production came forth . . . and production begat sales . . . and sales begat marketing . . . and marketing begat accounting . . . and accounting begat finance . . . and finance begat human resources . . . and human resources begat law . . . and law begat information technology. These clusters took root, emerged, grew, blossomed, and flourished unabated, and they multiplied into unique, isolated refuges for specialized experts to dwell and thrive in.

This tantalizing trend toward specialization had its genesis and approval in the higher levels' longing for control and consistency, and it flourished until it developed the potential to strangle the emergence and growth of new-found competitive imperatives like flexibility, spontaneity, and responsiveness. These isolated units began to speak in tongues (jargon) and protect their own secrets of information about the internal workings of the cluster and the tendencies of the customers. And it came to pass that procedures and practices aimed at solving consistency problems hardened and cemented these organizational methods and units. Specialization brought the sought-after subsystem efficiencies, but it also limited the scope of the organizations, chained them to the past, and bred an alarming degree of self-centeredness and rigidity. Alas, these organizational dwellings now face serious questions: Can we learn from the past without continuing to live there? Can we change the culture and structure of the organization to adapt to strategies aimed at satisfying current and future competitive imperatives?

> *Incomprehensible jargon is the hallmark of a profession.*
> —KINGMAN BREWSTER JR.[2]

## WHAT'S UP?

What's this current feeding frenzy around tearing down organizational silos? Is this another flavor-of-the-month change? A fad? By the way, why do we call them *silos?* Why don't we call functional departments chimneys? Or tubes? Or smokestacks? Or monuments? Or lighthouses?

### What Is a Silo, Anyway?

What is a silo and why does the term have such a negative connotation these days? To begin to unravel this mystery, we decided to start at the beginning.

We went to our trusty old *Random House Dictionary* and discovered two definitions for *silo*. A silo is "a tall, cylindrical structure in which grain is stored" or "a sunken shelter for storing and launching missiles." Hmm. Very interesting. So a silo is a valuable protector of precious materials, but a single-purpose, single-use, fragmented, isolated, fairly impenetrable piece of organizational architecture. Aha! Hold on. Look at that second definition—a sunken shelter for storing and launching missiles. Whoa! Missiles aimed and launched at what or whom? The competition? Other departments in the organization? The CEO? Curious. It would appear that the silo is indeed an intriguing metaphor, mostly descriptive of the downside of specialized activities within yesterday's and today's organizations.

## Don't Silos Have an Upside?

What about the upside? That grain and those missiles are valuable commodities and must be protected. If you tear down a grain silo, you expose the grain to the elements, the environment. You may lose the grain. If you tear out a missile silo, you may leave the organization defenseless. Is a silo also a gold mine? A fountain of knowledge? If we all became generalists, wouldn't we lose our specialized expertise? Wouldn't that loss create problems? At the very least, shouldn't we use a metaphor with an upside and a downside? Protection goes both ways—protecting the contents (professional employees) from the outside (the rest of the organization and the competitors) and protecting the outside from the contents.

> *Management must have the discipline not to keep pulling up the flowers to see if the roots are healthy.*
> —ROBERT TOWNSEND[3]

Maybe functional departments are just pastures with fences around them. But if so, when you tear down the fence, the cattle (employees) wander off and stray in harm's way, and you have to spend time and energy retrieving them. And then how do you keep them corralled when the fence is gone? And if they don't stay in the pasture, they may mingle with the sheep, pigs, or, heaven forbid, wolves. At the very least, won't they pick up bad habits by associating with the wrong people? At the worst, they might interbreed and produce jack-of-all-trades offspring. What happens to the expertise?

OK! Enough fun for now; let's get to the point! The real goals of tearing down those silos, are, of course, to maintain or enhance specific expertise while removing the walls and hopefully broadening the employees' perspective.

## OK. But Why Now?

It's easy enough to see how we got to where we are—specialization of labor, mass production, experts, efficiency! But why does it continue? What keeps those silos so vibrant in a changed milieu? Of what are these walls or fences made?

- Professional jargon

- Professional memberships

- Turf and resource protection

- Comfort zones

- Containment (to keep precious experts from getting contaminated by the unwashed)

- Discrimination

In a specialized professional department, is the employees' real allegiance to the company or to the profession? The answer might surprise you. Many managers we have worked with would privately state that it is the profession—do what the profession values and you won't have any trouble getting another job if and when you need one. In a university, many professors might choose their allegiance to their professional academy, not the university!

# FUNCTIONAL SYSTEMS AS POTENTIAL BARRIERS TO CHANGE

What do functions have to do with impeding organizational change anyway? Plenty! Functional silos can be formidable allies or formidable foes during the implementation of change. They have the potential to be either collaborative, coordinated components of a system in concert, or isolated, balkanized breeding grounds for self-interests—myopic cloning areas for training resisters.

There is nothing inherently wrong with grouping functional expertise. Specific knowledge can be a beautiful thing. But if the organization is ever going to reach its potential, that expertise must be carefully merged with the total organizational perspective. Employees must be able to understand decisions from the viewpoints of other functional areas. Sometimes they need to see decisions in terms of the business perspective, rather than the functional perspective. And organizations should reward employees for taking the broader perspective. For example, one hot topic these days is whether to increase IT representation in organizations to a higher level. Interesting question? Let's turn to our greatest business writer for help. Here's what Peter Drucker has to say about the peculiar role of IT and raising the status of the department: "As to the EDP function being placed on a higher level in the organization, that's a lot of bull____. I decide whether I want a washing machine. It's the mechanic's job to keep it running."

Yes! There is nothing wrong with IT. IT is an increasingly important function in the organization, much like accounting, finance, human resources, and law before it. What Drucker appears to be saying is that IT is (like finance, accounting, law, human resources, and the rest) a valuable staff or service function to the line activities (production, operations, and sales and marketing). We want to maintain and even enhance the expertise IT staff bring to the table while tearing down the walls and broadening their perspective, not encouraging them to narrow it further. In the broader business perspective—the company makes and sells washing machines! Everyone else's job is to help do that effectively and efficiently.

Production and sales (line functions at the heart of what a business does) are not immune to the pitfalls of functional silos. In fact, the gulf that exists because of disparate goals and turf battles between production and sales is probably the most common rift in many organizations. We've lost count of the number of times we've heard a manager mumble, "If we could only get production and sales to cooperate and coordinate!"

## Business Versus Functional Perspective

As a small example of the difference between a functional and a business perspective, consider the purchase of a ham at the local grocery store that you—for the purpose of argument—own and manage. What would you do if one of us bought a ham in your store and returned the next day with the ham to complain that it was not fresh and that he wanted a new one? The accounting perspective (functional expertise) might be that giving him another ham will cost $25 dollars. Why do it? The business perspective might be that $25 is not much to pay for a satisfied customer who spends thousands of dollars each year on groceries. Often, it isn't even the decision but the manner in which it is carried out that sticks with the customer. If you harass the customer, asking how he might have abused the ham—"When did you buy it? Was it ever in direct sunlight?"—and then reluctantly hand over another ham, he probably won't be back. Customers' time is valuable and they have better things to do than to abuse your hams.

## Who's Really at the Top of the Organizational Food Chain?

What is the most important group in the typical organization? Sounds like an easy question, right? Does it depend on the industry? The type of product or service? Is the answer the CEO and senior team? Perhaps. Are you talking short run or long run? In the short run, production (or operations) and sales are the two vital areas because on a day-to-day basis you have to make and sell stuff and provide valuable services.

With a touchy collective bargaining agreement approaching, or a concern for affirmative action or managing diversity, is it human resources? When you are in the middle of a gigantic, potentially crippling lawsuit over product liability, is the legal department the key? When you are midstream in the changeover to a new technological customer service system, is it IT? The point of this discussion is that, at any moment, any function could be the most important one. In fact, in many settings, any individual employee could be the key to success or failure. Value is determined by need. Value is also in the eye of the beholder. Value is circumstantial.

When an organization is really humming along, running in high gear, clicking on all cylinders, in the zone, the organization is operating as a holistic system. At any moment, the needed function takes the helm, steers everyone out of harm's way, and then relinquishes the helm.

## The Need for Committed Collaboration

Let's try another angle. Organizations don't have hearts, minds, and souls— people do! Organizations can be holistic, integrated systems, comprising interwoven components held together by the human element. In inorganic terms, organizations are tapestries. In organic terms, they are cells. This interconnectedness suggests that successfully implementing sizable change demands a coordinated effort from every function, working together, being on the same page—interactive, integrated, interdependent, counterdependent. When everyone is moving in the same direction, the whole can become greater than the sum of the parts. Synergy is a possible and necessary output of unity and input into successful change.

# SYNERGY IS MUSIC TO OUR EARS

Classical music offers a useful metaphor for the holistic approach to organizations. Even if you prefer another genre of music, hear us out on this. Have you ever seen and heard an exceptional symphony orchestra play a great piece of music? The total combination of strings, woodwinds, brass, and percussion instruments can be truly awe-inspiring. Many individual experts, playing a wonderful composition in concert, produce a marvelous product. On a smaller scale, the same thing applies to a great string quartet or a top-notch jazz band. But the symphony is larger, more diverse, and more complex, and therefore has the potential for a richer, fuller, more majestic sound.

> *The person who knows only one subject is almost as tiresome as the person who knows no subject.*
> —CHARLES DICKENS[5]

So what makes a great performance? The musical composition (comparable to the organizational vision, goals, and task)? The skill level of the collection of individual musicians (comparable to functional specialists)? The conductor (the change champion)? The instruments (the organization's equipment)? The acoustics (the work environment)? The audience (the customers)? Would the orchestra sound as good if the various musicians were on different floors? In separate buildings? In different countries? In silos?

We are not suggesting that you congregate your worldwide workforce in one room. What we *are* suggesting is that you approach the assignment of work in your organization from the business perspective, and that you arrange work around your business processes, not your functions. Perhaps you should form several different orchestras within your workforce. Let the composition (the organizational vision, goals, and task) determine the arrangement and interactions of each orchestra. Representative artists from different musical groupings (engineering, production, marketing, sales, customer service, human resources) should be teamed together for rehearsals and actual performances.

> *The musician who always plays on the same string is laughed at.*
> —HORACE[6]

What might hold disparate experts (employees) together? What is the glue? In a concert, the total orchestral performance is the goal (just as the organization should be judged by the overall goal). In a symphonic performance, the activities of individual musicians are tempered by rhythm

> *An expert is someone who knows more and more about less and less.*
> —NICHOLAS M. BUTLER[7]

(organizational pace and scheduling), dynamics (coordinated organizational movements), melody (prominence of the organizational theme), and the conductor (organizational leader).

In many organizations, the employee who plays on one string is rewarded and called an expert. In medicine, the specialist on the top half of the left ear has customers and makes money. We just hope you don't have abdominal pains while visiting this doctor.

## STRATEGIES TO TEAR DOWN THOSE SILOS

OK! But how can you tear down those silos—or at least chip away at them? Here are some suggestions for ways to begin to lower the walls.

- Where appropriate, use cross-functional work teams.

- Put a customer on each critical cross-functional team.

- Give bonuses to the best-performing cross-functional teams.

- Tie performance compensation to suprafunctional goals.

- Conduct cross-functional training and development.

- Use training and development to establish a common organizational language and perspective.

- Create a more appealing membership than the specialized groups.

- Conduct role reversals for key employees.

- Design exchanges (between functions) of a few key employees for six-month assignments.

- Discourage the use of jargon—insist on clarity.

- Promote people who think broadly.

- Connect everyone to customer satisfaction (total quality).

- When customers have trouble with a product or service, have the guilty individuals meet with the customer.

- Hire some new employees with broad business perspectives.

- Establish nonmanagerial career ladders tied to broader perspectives.

## THE BOTTOM LINE

Potential structural barriers to organizational change can be headed off using a two-pronged approach. First, attention must be paid to lowering the walls of functional silos by broadening the perspective of the specialists. Second, the organizational subsystems must be reviewed, redesigned, and aligned with the impending change. The work should be designed around the new critical business processes, not the functions. There is nothing sacred about organizational structure. Structure should support what you really do.

# Find the Needed Resources

*I gave him an unlimited budget and he exceeded it.*
—EDWARD BENNETT WILLIAMS[1]

In our opinion, the last potential hindrance to the successful implementation of a strategic change initiative is the supply of resources. Resource constraints can prevent the completion of the change on budget, on time, and on target. In any organization, you need stuff to get things done.

## RESOURCES ARE IN THE EYE OF THE BEHOLDER!

What are resources? Resources are often described as

- Anything of value
- Assets
- Budgets
- Capital

- Collateral

- Methods

- People

- Property

- Raw materials that get transformed into products

- Reserves

- Resourcefulness

- Stock

- Supplies you can draw upon

- The ways and means

- The wherewithal

From a practical standpoint, when you're leading change initiatives, resources are whatever you need to get the job done. So what are the available resources to accomplish the change? In organizations, we usually group resources into categories such as people, money, facilities, plant and equipment, supplies, time, knowledge, and information. You can have the right change, a great plan, and a clearly articulated case, but you still need the means to make it happen. Almost always, the obstacle is shortages—not enough resources to successfully complete the change implementation. It is no accident that assets are often referred to as scarce resources.

## I'M A LITTLE SHORT ON CASH (PEOPLE) AT THE MOMENT!

When was the last time you heard about a sponsor (someone leading a strategic initiative) praised for having too many people assigned to the project, too much capital in reserve, too much facility and equipment capacity, too much time in the forecast, too much knowledge, or too much information to ensure the unrestricted implementation of the assigned change? In this age of price sensitivity and internal competition for resources, it is far more likely that sponsors will encounter resource constraints and then receive criticism for being over time, off target, or off budget. In fact, it was not long ago that strategic initiatives were assigned to sponsors with no thought given to adding resources to the existing budgets. Great ideas about how to improve the organization were assigned on the "where there's a will there's a way!" premise. If you had the implementation of a strategic initiative dumped in your lap recently, maybe that's what you were told. We hope not.

> *About the time we think we can make ends meet, somebody moves the ends.*
> —HERBERT HOOVER[2]

When a company builds a plant, it allocates the people and funds needed. When it initiates a strategic initiative, the task is usually an add-on for the sponsor.

## BOTTOM-UP TO TOP-DOWN

Just as many organizations were beginning to recognize that strategic initiatives needed their own budget, a trend was developing that switched the way budgets were established. For a long time, corporate budgets were the result of rolling up all the income and expense projections submitted by all the supervisors and managers throughout the organization. There were painstaking efforts to find out from those closest to the work what the next twelve or eighteen months would cost for their area of responsibility. Once the numbers were added up, the CEO and CFO would manage final adjustments and communicate back down the organization.

In the past two decades, the budget process in most profit-oriented organizations has been turned upside down. The investment community has become more and more influential in setting profitability targets that should make shareholders happy and elevate the stock price. These profitability targets often drive the allocation of revenue forecasts and expense limits. Those closest to the work are asked to communicate the impact these financial requirements will have on operations. Said another way, they've been told, "Figure out how to meet this budget." And thus operating budgets and capital expenses are born again each year. This process generally provides some comfort, certainty, and security to upper management and investment bankers while giving headaches and heartburn to those lower in the organization.

Strategic planning and initiative planning get intertwined in this top-down financial process. Organizations begin by deciding on the important strategic initiatives that will position the business for future success. Then they have the task of planning the implementation of the initiatives. This task often results in an identification of resource requirements that are not included in forecasts and budgets. It is at this point that sponsors must mount a difficult and often awkward campaign. They must go upstream to sell top management on benefits and returns that will be worth the cost of implementation. This new dance is usually seen as realistic, but it unsettles top management's sense of security with the budget because strategic change always carries some risk that it may not pay off.

# ENLIGHTENED ORGANIZATIONS

We call organizations that budget for implementing initiatives "enlightened" because these are the ones where people can see! Organizations that have gone through enough cycles of identifying strategic changes, implementing plans, and evaluating results realize that positioning the business for the future needs resources. Implementation budgets have become part of their financial planning process. They have incorporated operating budgets, capital budgets, and initiative budgets into their total forecast.

Strategic initiative budgets need to account for a variety of resources:

- **People.** The initiative needs people to help design, develop, and install the change. A change initiative is usually a temporary assignment that sometimes includes outside contractors (outsourcing). One important area of conflict to watch out for is a scarce skill set that the organization needs both for ongoing work and for a strategic initiative: another example of how today competes with tomorrow.

- **Money.** There is no free lunch. One way or another, you have to pay for stuff. People's time doesn't come free. Tired people work slower and produce more defects.

- **Facilities.** To support implementation, you need dedicated space for storyboards, conference rooms, offices, warehousing, laboratories, scale-up plants, and the like. The last thing you should want a sponsor to have to spend time on is fighting for the appropriate facilities.

- **Equipment and supplies.** If a strategic initiative is truly strategic (or important) to future success, it will need the tools necessary for successful implementation. Equipment isn't cheap, even if you are just leasing it. If you are borrowing it, the political price can be even higher. Video-conferencing, surveys, computers, software, CAD/CAM equipment, manufacturing equipment, training programs, information resources, and so on support implementation success. The cost of these tools is often overlooked as additions to the cost of implementation.

- **Time.** Probably the most significant decision related to time is on-loan versus dedicated resources. Some strategic initiatives can be implemented with people who continue performing their full-time jobs and contribute to implementation on a temporary basis. Other initiatives need to receive full-time attention from all involved. It is not unusual for resources of people and time to need a perceptive and creative sponsor to develop workable schedules. Enlightened organizations want to know the scope and size of the resource requirements needed for implementation. When comprehensive resources have been identified and allocated, a sense of hope and reality takes hold. Without this positive picture, the sponsor often has some self-doubt that the change can realistically be accomplished.

- **Knowledge and information.** One resource is the knowledge base of the people who are implementing the strategic initiative. Skills, technical and human expertise, and change competencies are either advantages or drawbacks to successful completion. Mining the right intelligence (data and information) can also be costly.

The issue in today's economy (top-down budgeting driven by stock price) is that too often leadership evaluates sponsors by their creativity in figuring it out and making do. There is probably nothing wrong with wanting to have your cake and eat it too (implement the change at no additional cost), but it is rare in life to get both. As with most important changes there is a price to pay. Something will suffer. Also, the budget (or lack of one) for a strategic initiative sends a symbolic signal about the relative importance (or lack of importance) the initiative really has.

## GET CREATIVE

Even though change has a price tag, that does not mean that you should turn your back on the responsibility to think creatively about resource requirements for implementation.

In organizations that have a good track record for implementing strategic change, we have seen some extremely mature acts of creativity and teamwork. One organization, whose senior management team has been working on implementing strategic changes for three years, has learned that organizational success supersedes individual success. On this team, the members are all sponsors for at least two strategic initiatives every year. They are at a stage in their development where it is usual for three or four members of the team to volunteer for each strategic initiative even though they understand the challenges that implementation brings.

During the course of the year, this team dedicates half a day every month to monitoring progress on initiatives and solving rerailment problems. It is in these monthly meetings that you can see authentic acts of teamwork. For example, during one meeting, one team member reported having underestimated the number of people required for implementation. Another immediately spoke up and said, "I have an open requisition for a new hire that you can have. Your need is far more important than the job I want to fill." This insight was a genuine reflection of understanding the organization's strategic direction and sympathizing with the sponsor's dilemma to successfully complete a change. Now that's teamwork!

In another progress meeting with the same team, one of the sponsors reported the risk of derailing because of underestimated training and development costs. Once the issue was clear, another teammate offered some training money from his budget. "Just have the invoices sent to me. I'll take it out of my cost code." The priorities for the development costs became clear to all and they creatively took care of it within the family.

> *The best way to escape from a problem is to solve it.*
> —ANONYMOUS

They made no special requests to the corporation for extra funding. The team solved its own resource issues by having the maturity to understand the real priorities for success. This kind of creativity does not come easily; it is a result of hard work, plus attention to the discipline of leading strategic change.

## Strategies for Stretching Resources

If you don't have adequate resources to successfully complete the change, you may need to employ strategies to stretch the resources you do have. Here are some suggestions for using your available resources well:

- **Anticipate.** Start smart. Design the solution well from the beginning.

- **Beg, borrow.** Ask if you can share any existing people, supplies, equipment, facilities, or information.

- **Eliminate overlaps.** Reduce any redundancies in the implementation process.

- **Recruit wisely.** Get the most capable people onto your team or involved in its work from the start.

- **Spot opportunities.** Check the operating work for places where you can shift resources without major impact.

- **Work smarter.** Design an efficient process that eliminates duplication and waste.

## Strategies for Getting More Resources

If the possibility exists, obtain more resources for your initiative. Here are some suggestions:

- **Ask for what you need.** Evaluate your resource needs and request the resources necessary to accomplish the objective. Who knows? You might get them. One thing is sure—if you don't request what you need, you'll never know what might have happened.

- **Build credibility.** Plan an early success. Demonstrate the potential profits and savings.

- **Call in favors.** Use your IOUs to gain resources.

- **Integrate.** Link your change to another important initiative to increase your influence.

- **Locate potential investors.** Look for people who might want to get involved—either to support you or because the change might benefit their operations.

- **Promote your initiative.** Emphasize the importance and future profits and savings from the successful completion of your project.

- **Partner.** Form an alliance with resource-rich departments.

- **Start small.** Run a small-scale pilot program to test your process.

# THE BOTTOM LINE

On the one hand, the matter of resource requirements for implementation seems like a simple one. Do a good job of scoping resource needs and then either acquire them or abort the initiative. If the resources are unavailable, obviously the strategic initiative is not as important as it seemed when the decision to go forward was made. On the other hand, inadequate resources are often cited as the cause of failed implementation.

In our experience, all too often organizations want and need the results of the planned change, but they are unable or unwilling to allocate adequate resources for successful implementation. But this fact does not deter them from ordering the launch. Unfortunately, sponsors are put into a really tough situation. Sometimes they creatively win, but more often than not, the realities cause them to lose.

# Epilogue

# Practice the Art and Science of Leading Change

And so it goes. World without end! Leading change is difficult, complex, exciting—and rewarding when implementation is successful, on time, on target, and on budget. You have read this book because you are a student of change. You are perceptive. You are one of the people who cares about organizations, but—what is more important—you care about people. We do too!

Leading change is . . .

- Part art and part science
- Right brain and left brain
- Yin and yang
- *Logos* and *pathos*
- Big picture and details

We have attempted to share with you our understanding of the science of leading change and the art of leading change. The science is a little easier to grab. The science is represented in this book by the analytical building of the business case and the systematic minimization of the potential barriers to successful implementation. You should have a fairly good grasp of that by now.

The art of leading change is more ambiguous, but just as important. Selling the change story is part of the art form. Communication, motivation, and commitment are elements of the art form, too. The art is the human, personal, interactive, passionate, emotional side of leading change. Your leadership skills will be tested to their fullest. Figure 5 is our attempt to put a face on the total package needed for successfully leading change. Use your imagination! Dream big! Do great things! Our organizations need more people like you!

FIGURE 5
## The Art and Science of Leading Change

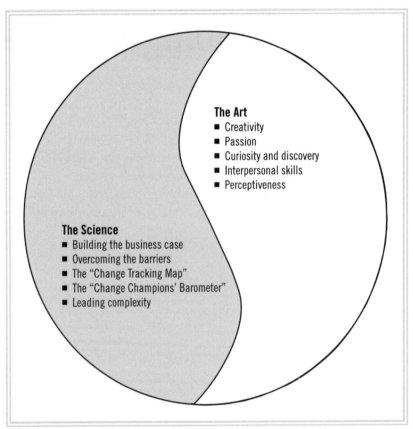

**The Art**
- Creativity
- Passion
- Curiosity and discovery
- Interpersonal skills
- Perceptiveness

**The Science**
- Building the business case
- Overcoming the barriers
- The "Change Tracking Map"
- The "Change Champions' Barometer"
- Leading complexity

# APPENDIX

## PACK YOUR ACTION TOOL KIT

This appendix contains a condensed action tool resource kit with three main components. First, the "Change Tracking Map" summarizes the book in an easy-to-use and easy-to-remember form. Second, the "Change Tracking Planner" gives you a tool you can reproduce and use for each change you implement. Third and last, the "Change Champions' Barometer" will help you assess your chances for a successful implementation. The barometer gives you a way to gauge what you're doing. It's not a tested, scientific measurement; treat it as an amusing guesstimate, an indicator that can provoke further thought about assuring successful implementation.

## CHANGE TRACKING MAP

The following charts provide a quick road map of the changes discussed in the book. Use this map as a checklist or reference, reviewing the indicated chapters if you need more information.

## Sources of Change (Chapter 2)

### External Drivers

| Competitive/Customer | Technological | Social/Economic/Regulatory |
|---|---|---|
| ■ Intelligence research | ■ Scientific breakthroughs | ■ Demographic trends |
| ■ Buyer behavior trends | ■ Information systems | ■ Worker supply issues |
| ■ Currency fluctuations | ■ E-commerce | ■ Industry legislation |
| ■ Customer value search | ■ Faster, cheaper transportation and communication | ■ Regional trade agreements |
| ■ Capital market pressures | | ■ Regulation/deregulation |
| ■ Emerging markets | ■ Intellectual property issues | ■ Workforce diversity |
| ■ E-commerce | ■ Internet/intranets | ■ Terrorism |
| ■ Global markets and competition | ■ Manufacturing process innovations | |
| ■ Labor costs/supply/ replacement | ■ Miniaturization | |

## Competitive Advantage (Chapter 3)

| Differentiation | | | Scale | |
|---|---|---|---|---|
| Customer Service | Product Attributes | Market Niche | Cost Orientation | Market Dominance |
| GOAL | GOAL | GOAL | GOAL | GOAL |
| Customer loyalty | Price premium | Unique market segment leader | Low-cost provider | Market shaper |

| Internal Fitness (Chapter 4) | | | |
|---|---|---|---|
| **Strategic Leadership** | **Customer Value** | **People and Culture** | **Technology** |
| ▪ Competitive analysis<br>▪ Mission and values<br>▪ Goals and strategies<br>▪ Financial management<br>▪ Strategic initiatives<br>▪ Management of change<br>▪ Continuous monitoring | ▪ Customer requirements<br>▪ Product development<br>▪ Quality production processes<br>▪ Lean production<br>▪ Supplier relations<br>▪ Benchmarking<br>▪ Supply chain management | ▪ Productivity<br>▪ Strategic alignment<br>▪ Teamwork<br>▪ Reward systems<br>▪ Creativity and innovation<br>▪ Learning organization | ▪ Data warehousing and mining<br>▪ Customer information systems<br>▪ Management information systems<br>▪ Equipment<br>▪ Communication systems<br>▪ E-commerce |

| Type of Change (Chapter 6) | | |
|---|---|---|
| **Developmental** | **Opportunistic** | **Transformational** |
| ▪ Internal fitness<br>▪ Evolutionary<br>▪ Planned<br>▪ High involvement | ▪ External drivers<br>▪ Short window of time<br>▪ Sizing and seizing<br>▪ Low involvement | ▪ Competitive advantage<br>▪ Revolutionary<br>▪ Organic<br>▪ Total involvement |
| **Examples of Management Practices, Programs, Strategies, and Techniques** | | |
| ▪ Training and development<br>▪ Performance feedback<br>▪ Reward and recognition systems<br>▪ Strong project management<br>▪ Quality teams | ▪ Quick advance preparation<br>▪ Comprehensive product development processes<br>▪ Nimble opportunity assessment processes<br>▪ Capacity to tolerate stress | ▪ Compelling vision for the future<br>▪ Reward and recognition systems that support the change<br>▪ Test-drive change<br>▪ Open meetings and conferences<br>▪ Multiple champions<br>▪ "Letting go" rituals |

## Assessing the Consistency of the Change with the Work Culture (Chapter 7)

### Alignment of Business Strategy with Culture

| Customer Service | Product Attributes | Cost Orientation | Market Dominance |
|---|---|---|---|
| ▪ Employee loyalty | ▪ Invention | ▪ Control | ▪ Growth |
| ▪ Teamwork | ▪ Freedom | ▪ Reliability | ▪ Aggressiveness |
| ▪ Relationships | ▪ Individual | ▪ Predictability | ▪ Strength |
| ▪ Sensitivity | ▪ Diversity | ▪ Accuracy | ▪ Knowledge |
| ▪ Consensus | ▪ Achievement | ▪ Continuous improvement | ▪ Quickness |

### If the change is inconsistent with the culture:

- Change the change.
- Plan on slowing the implementation process.
- Reshape the work culture to support the change.
- Prepare for marginal short-term results (failure).

## Five Key Implementation Issues

| Potential Obstacles | Helpful Strategies |
|---|---|
| **Cultural Roadblocks (Chapter 7)** | |
| • Degree of inflexibility | • Measure and reward new behaviors. |
| • Stuck in old ways | • Set new hiring criteria. |
| • Global differences | • Make sure all managers adopt and model the new behavior. |
| • Poor implementation history | • Publicize new metrics and business results. |
| **Individual Resistance (Chapter 8)** | |
| • Perceived threats | • Encourage expression of resistance. |
| • Fears and uncertainty | • Address personal ("me") issues quickly. |
| • Conflicts | • Share information, clarify, and support. |
| • Distrust | • Involve resisters in solution development. |
| • Different perceptions | |
| • Habits | |
| **Inadequate Sponsorship (Chapter 9)** | |
| • Lack of sponsor credibility | • Communicate broadly. |
| • Lack of leadership commitment | • Plan well, secure resources, monitor progress. |
| • Political and turf issues | • Provide training where necessary. |
| • Lack of support | • Change your own behavior. |
| **System Constraints (Chapter 10)** | |
| • Financial and budgeting | • Protect quality, customer service, and profitability. |
| • Compensation and reward | • Build a manual system. |
| • Computer and information | • Use your informal network. |
| • Manufacturing and production | • Find ways to leverage the existing system. |
| **Resource Constraints (Chapter 11)** | |
| • Financial | • Don't let constraints become a convenient excuse. |
| • Physical | • Brainstorm new possibilities. |
| • Informational | • Look for allies and joint ventures. |
| • Human | • Ask for what you need. |

## Leading Change

### Develop Yourself

- Keep well informed about the research on change winners and losers.
- Understand the paradox of long-range effectiveness versus short-range efficiency and find ways to accomplish both.
- Assess the impact of work culture on the speed of implementation and factor it into your action plan timing.
- Build internal capability so as to increase speed.
- Understand the psychology of resistance and develop better listening skills.
- Learn project management processes and apply with mastery.
- Know when to empower and when to not empower.
- Practice, try new ideas, and observe lessons.
- Keep well informed, develop skill, and master the art of change leadership.

## Custom Handbook
Create a unique implementation plan
by using the Change Tracking Planner

| Change Plan Element | Value of Element |
| --- | --- |
| The Business Case | **Rationale:** Explains the reason for change, its scope and payback |
| The Compelling Change Story | **Motivation:** Solicits positive reaction and initial commitment from the "change targets" |
| Type Assesssment | **Approach:** Charts a "mind-set" before we begin to craft an implementation plan |
| Culture Assessment | **Speed:** Helps gauge a realistic pace and speed for milestone deadlines |
| Roadblock Assessment | **Anticipation:** Creates solutions to reduce or prevent resistance and other roadblocks |
| Milestone Plan | **Rerailing:** Supports the detection of derailment and enables quicker rerailing action |
| Sponsor Behavior | **Role Model:** Serves as a reminder to practice the implementation skillsw and behavior that will support success |

# CHANGE TRACKING PLANNER

Reproduce this form and use it as a planner for every change you make. You can use the chapter references to look back at the information for each section.

---

### Define the Change to Be Implemented

Name the Change: _____

Sponsor: _____

Measurable Objective of the Change: _____

_____

_____

| **Other Functions Affected** | **To What Degree** |
| --- | --- |
| 1. _____ | ____ high ____ medium ____ low |
| 2. _____ | ____ high ____ medium ____ low |
| 3. _____ | ____ high ____ medium ____ low |

Required Completion Date: _____

Budget: _____

---

## What Is Causing This Change? (Chapters 2, 3, and 4)

| Check the Sources | Provide a detailed explanation of the reasons this change should be implemented. |
|---|---|
| **External Driver**<br>■ Competition<br>■ Customers<br>■ Technological advancements<br>■ Social trends<br>■ Economic cycles<br>■ Regulatory pressures | |
| **Competitive Advantage**<br>■ Customer service<br>■ Product attributes<br>■ Market niche<br>■ Cost orientation<br>■ Market dominance | |
| **Internal Fitness**<br>■ Strategic leadership<br>■ Customer value<br>■ People and culture<br>■ Technological infrastructure | |

## What is the compelling change story? (Chapter 5)

### Why is it right? (Cost, benefit, justified risk)

### Crafting a Compelling Presentation

List the titles of your overhead slides (see the four action steps in Chapter 6).

1. _____
2. _____
3. _____
4. _____
5. _____
6. _____
7. _____
8. _____
9. _____
10. _____
11. _____
12. _____
13. _____
14. _____
15. _____

16. _____
17. _____
18. _____
19. _____
20. _____
21. _____
22. _____
23. _____
24. _____
25. _____
26. _____
27. _____
28. _____
29. _____
30. _____

## What type of change is this? (Chapter 6)

| Developmental Change | Opportunistic Change | Transformational Change |
|---|---|---|

What practices, programs, strategies, and management techniques will help you most during implementation?

_____

_____

_____

## Is this change consistent with your current work culture? (Chapter 7)

If not, how will you adjust your implementation plan?

_____

_____

_____

## Anticipating Implementation Issues (Chapters 7–11)

### Which of these common roadblocks do you expect to encounter?

- Inadequate sponsorship
- Individual resistance
- Cultural roadblocks
- System constraints
- Resource constraints
- Other

| Describe the issue. | How will you creatively avoid or overcome the roadblocks? |
|---|---|
| _____ | _____ |
| _____ | _____ |
| _____ | _____ |

## Implementation Plan (Chapter 8)

| Action Steps and Milestones | Responsibility | Deadline |
|---|---|---|
| _____ | _____ | _____ |
| _____ | _____ | _____ |
| _____ | _____ | _____ |

How will you know when the implementation of this change is over? (What are your measurable deliverables?)

## Effective Leadership (Chapters 9, 10, and 11)

**Development Plan:** What do you want to learn, practice, and improve as a result of sponsoring implementation?

_____

_____

_____

## Identifying Organizational Factors

**Directions:** Examine each organizational factor on the left as it relates to your change. Will this factor apply to your change (yes or no)? Record the total number of yes answers in each category at the bottom of the right-hand columns. Subtract the number of unfavorable yes's from the favorable ones to get your potential for successful change.

| Favorable Organizational Factors | Will This Factor Apply? (Yes or No) |
| --- | --- |
| 1. Visible sponsor support throughout | _____ |
| 2. Adequately staffed and funded | _____ |
| 3. Dedicated and capable project team | _____ |
| 4. Strong project manager | _____ |
| 5. High organizational priority | _____ |
| 6. Progress tracked and published | _____ |
| 7. Reasons for the change clear to all | _____ |
| 8. Executive support for sponsor | _____ |
| 9. Objective specific and time oriented | _____ |
| 10. Rewards for change and innovation | _____ |
| 11. Organizational culture supportive of change and innovation | _____ |
| **Total number of Yes's** | _____ |

| Unfavorable Organizational Factors | Will This Factor Apply? (Yes or No) |
|---|---|
| 12. No clear, credible sponsor | _____ |
| 13. Lack of support from top management | _____ |
| 14. Sponsor ambivalent or departed | _____ |
| 15. Too many competing changes and priorities | _____ |
| 16. No understanding of the need for change | _____ |
| 17. Problems not communicated to sponsor | _____ |
| 18. Change clashes with the culture | _____ |
| 19. Resources diverted to other activities | _____ |
| 20. Support systems don't deliver | _____ |
| 21. Increased workloads without rewards | _____ |
| 22. Organization has a bad history of managing change | _____ |
| **Total number of Yes's** | _____ |
| **Potential for success =** | _____ |

### Interpreting Your "Potential for Success" Score

Remember, this is just for fun. For a little insight cloaked in levity, you can loosely interpret your score as follows:

- A large positive number (6–11) = You've got it made! Success is a done deal!
- A small positive number (2–5) = A good chance for success if you fix a few things.
- A washout (+1, 0, –1) = This change could go either way—lots of shoring up needed!
- A small negative number (–2 to –5) = The odds are against success, but . . .
- A large negative number (–6 to –11) = Yikes! This change seems doomed!

Hopefully, this exercise has helped you learn some things about change. As Kurt Lewin (the originator of force-field analysis for change) suggests, any change always has forces working for it and forces working against it. How do they stack up for you now? What might you need to do to reduce the unfavorable factors? Increase the favorable factors? Feel free to change the factors in this action tool. Customize both lists (favorable and unfavorable factors) to fit your organization and industry. But be honest—don't stack the deck in your favor!

# CHANGE CHAMPIONS' BAROMETER

**Directions:** Answer the following questions by placing the number that corresponds to your answer (1, 2, or 3) in the space in the rating column to the right. Add the numbers in the rating column to get your total score.

## How much is known about this change?

1 = Vague direction and intent have been developed.

2 = Concrete definition and outcomes have been established, but resource requirements and risks are ambiguous.

3 = Definition, resources, outcomes, and risks are understood.

Clarity Rating

_____

## How compelling is this change? What is driving it?

1 = Internal fitness

2 = Competitive advantage

3 = External drivers

Compelling Rating

_____

## How difficult is this change to manage?

1 = Transformational

2 = Opportunistic

3 = Developmental

Type Rating

_____

## How consistent is this change with the current work culture?

1 = Behavior required by the change is opposite to current behavior.

2 = Behavior required is somewhat different from current behavior.

3 = Behavior required by this change is consistent with current behavior.

Culture Rating

_____

## How much push-back do you expect?

1 = Anticipate three or more roadblocks.

2 = Anticipate two roadblocks.

3 = Anticipate one roadblock.

Roadblock Rating

_____

## How experienced is the leader of this change?

1 = This is the sponsor's first strategic initiative to implement.

2 = The sponsor has implemented one other strategic initiative.

3 = The sponsor has implemented two or more strategic initiatives.

Sponsorship Rating

_____

**Total Score**                  _____

## Graphing the Barometer

**Directions:** Transfer your scores from pages 163–164 to each of the six areas in the "Change Profile" section. The closer your numbers are to the center of the wheel, the tougher the change. Check to see where your total score falls in the "Leadership Challenge" (page 166) to see how close you are to a green light for your planned change.

### Change Profile

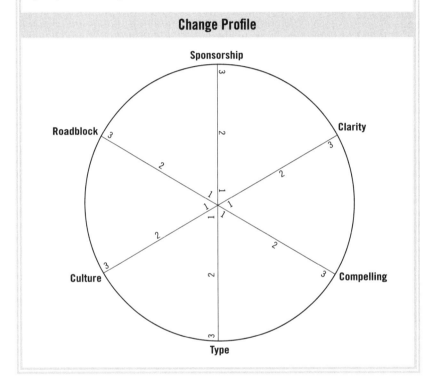

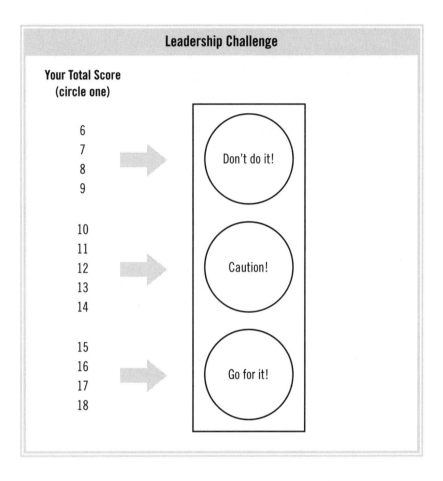

# NOTES

## PREFACE

1. *USA Today,* November 23, 1999, p. 5D.

## CHAPTER 1

1. American news reporter and commentator (1912–1992).
2. British novelist and prime minister (1804–1881); this quote was taken from a speech delivered in Edinburgh, Scotland (October 29, 1867).
3. Organizational metaphors such as machines and organisms were first discussed in Gareth Morgan's *Images of Organizations* (see 2nd ed.; Thousand Oaks, Calif.: Sage, 1997).
4. American business philosopher, author, and educator (1909– ).
5. The source for this quote was Robert Staughton Lynd and Helen Merrell Lynd, *Middletown* (New York: Harcourt, Brace, 1929), part VI, chapter 29.
6. Indian nationalist leader (1869–1948).
7. CEO, Cisco Systems (1951– ).
8. American automobile manufacturer (1863–1947).

## PART 1 INTRODUCTION

1. Richard Bloom, "Round 2: Wal-Mart Versus Costco," *Globe and Mail* (Toronto).
2. English journalist and author (1874–1936).

## CHAPTER 2

1. Founder and CEO, Dell Computer Corporation (1965– ).
2. Our categories for external pressures are an expansion and different slicing of the external components suggested in W. Warner Burke, *Organization Change: Theory and Practice* (Thousand Oaks, Calif.: Sage, 2002), pp. 283–285, and Ricky Griffin, *Management* (Boston: Houghton Mifflin, 2005), pp. 404–405.
3. President, Xerox Corporation (1938– ).
4. Chairman and editor in chief, *U.S. News and World Report* (1937– ).
5. American disc jockey and music industry executive.

## CHAPTER 3

1. This table is an enhancement of the original competitive advantage model in Michael E. Porter, *Competitive Advantage: Creating and Sustaining Superior Performance* (New York: Free Press, 1985). Revised and reprinted with permission.
2. Chairman emeritus, Neiman-Marcus Department Stores.
3. American essayist and poet (1803–1882).
4. President, Colgate-Palmolive Company (1909– ).
5. American businessman (1852–1919).
6. American consumer advocate (1934– ).
7. American actor and comedian (1937– ).
8. Chairman and CEO, PepsiCo, Inc. (1935– ).
9. Pierre Mourier and Martin Smith, *Conquering Organizational Change* (Atlanta: CEP Press, 2001), p. 19.

## CHAPTER 4

1. Great hockey player.
2. We were introduced to the idea that speed is a by-product of skill by E. Paul Dickenson, a high-performance driving instructor whose firm is E. Paul, Inc.
3. American educator and business writer (1925– ).
4. American business writer and educator (1942– ).
5. American film producer and entrepreneur (1901–1966).
6. American psychologist and author (1908–1970).
7. This theory was presented by Dr. Patrick Williams, a professor at Pepperdine University, as part of his "Total Systems Model."

## CHAPTER 5

1. American critic and publicist.
2. American poet (1819–1892).
3. American journalist (1853–1937).
4. American author, judge, and toastmaster (twentieth century).
5. Indian nationalist leader (1869–1948).
6. These suggested openings are a mixture of our thoughts and a few suggestions found in the following sources: Scot Ober, *Contemporary Business Communication*, 2nd ed. (Boston: Houghton Mifflin, 1995), p. 464, and Louis E. Boone, David L. Kurtz, and Judy R. Block, *Contemporary Business Communication* (Englewood Cliffs, N.J.: Prentice Hall, 1994), pp. 453–455.
7. Albert Mehrabian, *Nonverbal Communication* (Chicago: Aldine, 1972).

8. The action steps and Table 5 are major revisions of materials originally presented in Ken Matejka and Diane Ramos, *Hook 'Em: Speaking and Writing to Catch and Keep a Business Audience* (New York: AMACOM, 1996).

## PART 2 INTRODUCTION

1. Malcolm Gladwell, *The Tipping Point: How Little Things Can Make a Big Difference* (New York: Little, Brown, 2000).

## CHAPTER 6

1. American twentieth-century author.
2. Our discussion of the types of change builds on our own experience and on Mintzberg's distinction between "deliberate" and "emergent" strategies. See H. Mintzberg, "Crafting Strategy," *Harvard Business Review* 65 (July–August 1987): 66–75. We also draw on Orlikowski and Hofman's introduction of "opportunity-based change," found in W. Orlikowski and J. Hofman, "An Improvisational Model for Change Management: The Case of Groupware Technologies," *Sloan Management Review* 38, no. 2 (Winter 1997): 11–21.
3. Greek philosopher (384–322 B.C.).
4. Robert H. Miles and Associates, *The Organizational Life Cycle* (San Francisco: Jossey-Bass, 1980).
5. Former CEO, Coca-Cola Company (1931–1997).
6. For a more complete discussion and explanation of opportunistic patterns, see Adrian J. Slywotzky and David J. Morrison, *Profit Patterns: Thirty Ways to Anticipate and Profit from Strategic Forces Shaping Your Business* (New York: Times Business–Random House, 1999).
7. Spanish painter and sculptor (1881–1973).
8. Greek philosopher (540–480 B.C.).

## CHAPTER 7

1. Professor emeritus, University of Richmond, Virginia.
2. T. E. Deal and A. A. Kennedy, *Corporate Cultures: The Rites and Rituals of Corporate Life* (Reading, Mass.: Addison-Wesley, 1982), p. 4.
3. E. H. Schein, "The Role of the Founder in Creating Organizational Culture," *Organizational Dynamics* (Summer 1983): 14.
4. Thomas J. Peters and Robert H. Waterman Jr., *In Search of Excellence: Lessons from America's Best-Run Companies* (New York: HarperCollins, 1982), p. 103.

5. Business executive, author, motivational speaker.

6. Retired CEO of IBM (1942– ). From his *Who Says Elephants Can't Dance?* (New York: Harper Business, 2002), p. 182.

7. John F. Kennedy (1917–1963) was the 35th president of the United States (1961–1963).

8. For an explanation of "deep structures," see C. J. Gersick, "Revolutionary Change Theories: A Multilevel Exploration of the Punctuated Equilibrium Paradigm," *Academy of Management Review* 16 (1991): 10–36.

9. Roman emperor (63 B.C.–A.D. 14).

10. Writer, actor, and filmmaker (1935– ).

11. Philosopher and writer (1817–1862).

## CHAPTER 8

1. American business author and educator, Harvard University.

2. American statesman and philosopher (1706–1790).

3. This model for categorizing the workforce into three groups in terms of their reactions to change was first introduced in Ken Matejka and Richard J. Dunsing, *A Manager's Guide to the Millennium* (New York: AMACOM, 1995), pp. 32–33.

4. British statesman and prime minister (1874–1965).

5. American actor and humorist (1879–1935).

6. The individual resistance factors and strategies found in this section represent our own experiences, supplemented by some suggestions found in these sources: Robert Heller, *Managing Change* (New York: DK Publishing, 1998); Pierre Mourier and Martin Smith, *Conquering Organizational Change* (Atlanta: CEP Press, 2001); Clark Gilbert and Joseph Bower, "Disruptive Change," *Harvard Business Review* (May 2002): 95–104, and Ricky Griffin, *Management* (Boston: Houghton Mifflin, 2005), pp. 409–410.

7. American humorist (1818–1885).

8. Scottish author (1918– ).

9. Chairman, Ford Motor Company (1920– ).

10. Mark Twain is the pen name of Samuel Clemens, American author (1835–1910).

11. The remainder of this chapter is a revised and updated version of an original article: Ken Matejka and Bill Presutti, "Rebuilding the Survivor's Loyalty," *Management Decision* 26, no. 6 (1988): 56–57. Reprinted with permission. See http://www.emeraldinsight.com/md.htm.

12. American race car driver (1951– ).

## CHAPTER 9

1. W. W. Burke and N. W. Biggart, "Interorganizational Relations," in *Enhancing Organizational Performance,* edited by D. Druckman, J. E. Singer, and H. Van Cott (Washington, D.C.: National Academy Press, 1997), pp. 120–149.
2. Pierre Mourier and Martin Smith, *Conquering Organizational Change* (Atlanta: CEP Press, 2001), p. 197.
3. Elisabeth Kübler-Ross, *On Death and Dying* (New York: Touchstone Books, 1997).
4. William Bridges, *Transitions: Making Sense of Life's Changes* (Reading, Mass.: Addison-Wesley, 1980).
5. President and CEO, American Management Association (1895–1971).

## CHAPTER 10

1. American author (1919–1990).
2. President of Yale University and U.S. ambassador to Britain (1919–1988).
3. American business writer and former president of Avis Rent-a-Car (1920–1998).
4. American business philosopher, author, and educator (1909– ).
5. English author (1812–1870).
6. Roman poet and satirist (65–08 B.C.).
7. American educator and Nobel Laureate (1862–1947).

## CHAPTER 11

1. Edward Bennett Williams was the owner of the Washington Redskins. He made this remark about coach George Allen.
2. Herbert Hoover (1874–1964) was the 31st president of the United States.

# INDEX